A Collection of New Testament Essays
For the encouragement of those
with 'ears to hear'

John Belham

PARVA PRESS

Copyright © 2025 by John Belham

All rights reserved. No part of this publication may be reproduced, distributed or transmitted in any form or by any means, without prior written permission.

Parva Press
E-mail: parvapress@lords-prayer.co.uk

Principal Scripture quotations are from the ESV* Bible (The Holy Bible, English Standard Version*) copyright © 2001 by Crossway, a publishing ministry of Good News Publishers. Used by permission. All rights reserved.

Supporting references marked RSV and some allusions are drawn from the Revised Standard Version of the Bible, Copyright 1952 (2nd edition 1971) by the Division of Christian Education of the National Council of the Churches of Christ in the United States of America. Used by Permission. All rights re-served.

Book Layout © 2017 BookDesignTemplates.com
Manuscript inspiration REB
Cover Design and Layout SJB.

British Library Cataloguing in Publication Data.
A catalogue record for this publication is available from the British Library.

ISBN 978-0-9537489-7-6

To the glory of God
and the stirring, strengthening
and encouragement of his people

"He who has ears to hear, let him hear"
Mark 4:9

CONTENTS

Introduction and Acknowledgements 1
The Key to the Gospel 3
The Call of Matthew 5
Praying to the Father 13
The Woman of Samaria 19
Zacchaeus 29
She has done what she could 37
The Triumphal Entry into Jerusalem 45
Encounter with Pilate 53
Aspects of the Cross 61
Thomas 71
Pentecost Then and Now 79
The Trinity 87
Paul in Athens 93
Paul in Corinth 101
The Christian Church in Danger 109
Righteousness, Peace and Joy 115
Looking to Jesus 123
The Circumstances of our Lord's Promised Return 131
About the Cover Image, the Author and related Publications 139

Introduction and Acknowledgements

The subtitle is taken from a challenge Jesus often gave the great crowds as he taught them, 'He who has ears to hear, let him hear.' It was a challenge that recognised that there would be those among his hearers who found his words interesting but were left quite untouched, those who found their 'hearts strangely warmed', and yet others who would react with hardened hearts and criticism.

Acknowledging that much the same can be true of the written word, the prayer of the author for those who read these essays is that the Lord God would stir, strengthen and encourage those to whom he has given 'ears to hear'.

My grateful thanks is due to those who helped with the production of this volume, to the writers of the New Testament and supremely to the One about whom they wrote.

The Key to the Gospel

The Son of Mary – Who is he?

The child laid in a manger, the babe of Bethlehem, Mary's firstborn son was no ordinary child. He was the 'salvation and consolation of Israel' – long sought by Simeon and Anna. (Luke 2:22-35) He was the 'One born king of the Jews', as he was described by the visiting Magi, much to Herod's alarm. (Matthew 2:1-12) He was the 'prophet of Nazareth' who 'went about doing good'. . . And yet he was 'despised and rejected' by the religious leaders and ultimately crucified with criminals.

But who was he, and why should we, at such a great distance in time and geography, be concerned about him? Why is the son of Mary so significant?

Many people accept and highly regard Jesus as one of the great religious leaders of the world, a good man and great moral teacher.

However, by his words and by his deeds, Jesus showed himself to be to be far more than that. The prophets of the Old Testament, and the New Testament writers bear witness to the Lord Jesus being the Son of God; the long-promised Messiah, the Anointed One, the Christ, the Lord God among us in a fully human body.

Isaiah speaks of a child being born of a virgin, whose name will be Emanuel, 'God with us', a child who will bear titles that no mere human could ever fulfil: 'Mighty God', 'Everlasting Father',

'Prince of Peace', One whose kingdom will never cease. (Isaiah 7:14 and 9:6-7)

The apostle Paul writes, 'In the fullness of time, God sent forth his Son, born of a woman, born under the law' – Paul is describing the Son of God, yet born a human being, a Jewish person. (Galatians 4:4)

At the conclusion of his gospel the apostle John writes, 'Now Jesus did many other signs in the presence of the disciples, which are not written in this book; but these are written that you may believe that Jesus is the Christ, the Son of God, and that believing you may have life in his name.' (John. 20:30-3, see also John. 1:1-14 and 3:16)

Despite the frequent fulfilment of their own Scriptures and the witness of their own eyes and ears, his being the Son of God and the true Messiah or Christ was the very thing that the religious leaders of Jesus' day rejected.

The Call of Matthew

After this he [Jesus] went out and saw a tax-collector named Levi, sitting at the tax booth. And he said to him, "Follow me." And leaving everything, he rose and followed him.

And Levi made him a great feast in his house; and there was a large company of tax-collectors and others reclining at table with them. And the Pharisees and their scribes grumbled at his disciples, saying, "Why do you eat and drink with tax-collectors and sinners?" And Jesus answered them, "Those who are well have no need of a physician, but those who are sick. I have not come to call the righteous but sinners to repentance.'

And they said to him, "The disciples of John fast often and offer prayers, and so do the disciples of the Pharisees, but yours eat and drink." And Jesus said to them, "Can you make wedding-guests fast while the bridegroom is with them? The days will come when the bridegroom is taken away from them, and then they will fast in those days."

Luke 5:27-35 English Standard Version

The Call of Matthew

Matthew was also known as Levi. He was a tax collector – collecting taxes, which were not to be used for the good of the whole society; these were taxes demanded by the Roman overlords, the people's hated conquerors.

Levi or Matthew was sitting receiving customs. Matthew's gospel tells he was in Capernaum, a town on the main road from Damascus to the Mediterranean seaport of Acre. Almost certainly he would have been collecting a toll charge on all goods passing along that stretch of the road, and doing so for Herod Antipas, the Roman governor of the area. Tax collectors were richly rewarded from the taxes they collected, but they were despised and loathed by their fellow countrymen as traitors and thieves.

Had Matthew heard about the forthcoming Messiah from John the Baptist? Had he heard about him from local people? Capernaum was Jesus' 'home city' and base. We don't know. But in some way the Lord God had prepared Matthew's heart for this call of Jesus to follow him, and he was ready to respond. The Lord God has many ways of preparing the hearts and minds of those he has chosen. Matthew readily obeyed. He was eager to learn more, and not just selfishly. He wanted his colleagues to hear too, so he arranged for a meal – a feast, says Luke.

The people who gathered at Matthew's table were not the 'nicest' or the 'most respectable' of people – they were tax collectors and sinners. It was a meal of welcome for Jesus and his disciples, and for Matthew and his colleagues to meet and to hear the Lord Jesus.

A meal with controversy

Matthew's meal did not delight the scribes and Pharisees, who were never far away, just 'keeping an eye on things'. So they asked the disciples something like this, 'If you wish to keep yourselves 'pure' and 'acceptable', like us, and are aiming to win the favour of God by carefully obeying every command he has given, as we are – what are you doing eating with such defiled, contaminated and fallen people?' 'Why are you following a man who mixes and even eats with such people? He cannot be a holy man, worth following, let alone God's true Messiah!'

And further, 'This is no time to feast. This is a season for religious prayer and fasting.' (Mark's Gospel tells us that the Pharisees and John the Baptist's followers were fasting at this time.)

The accusations were directly and indirectly slurs against the Lord Jesus. And Jesus answered them saying, essentially, 'You have got it completely the wrong way round. Sharing the good news of the kingdom of heaven with people who need to hear it, must take priority over your man-made rules and religious observances.'

Religion and religious observance, as an end in itself, can be a joyless thing. But as Psalm 16 verse 11 tells us, 'in the presence of God there is fullness of joy.' Emmanuel, 'God among us', was present among his chosen Jewish people. The scribes and Pharisees had just witnessed the amazing healing of a totally paralysed man; the man let down through the roof. (The account of this is found in the earlier verses of Luke chapter five.) Yet they were not willing to see or acknowledge who the Lord Jesus truly was. However, the disciples, the ordinary people and the despised tax collectors and sinners were willing – and there was awe and wonder and joy in the presence of the Lord Jesus, like the joy of a wedding.

One day, as he warned, he would be taken from them. The Greek word suggests snatched away violently – was this perhaps a glimpse of his forthcoming arrest and crucifixion at the hands of the religious leaders? Then, but not till then, will his disciples fast. Then, as Matthew Henry puts it, 'with their hearts full of sorrow, their hands full of work, and the world full of enmity and rage against them,' then they will fast. (As we read they did – Acts 13:2)

A meal with a purpose
Like his fellow tax collectors, Matthew was a rich man, and he provided this feast at his own expense. Why did he do it?

Everyone hated the tax collectors, but the Lord Jesus had 'bothered' with Matthew. He had chosen him and called him to be one of his disciples, saying simply, "Follow me," and, as we've seen, under the hand of God, he did.

Matthew wanted to hear and learn more and he wanted others to meet and hear Jesus too. A great deal of good work for the Lord is done over a meal – as our circumstances permit. Especially so, when like Matthew, we invite the Lord Jesus to be present and take the lead. For Matthew it was a meal with a purpose.

For the Lord Jesus too, it was a meal with a purpose, 'to call sinners to repentance'. It was an opportunity, not for polite, respectable, light conversation, but an opportunity to call these precious but straying people, not to live their lives as their own inclinations drove them, but to live in God's world for the Lord God – to love him and honour him and joyfully serve him. And that is what repentance is all about.

Our Lord used three words which we easily pass over because we don't have cause to use them in everyday business or as we shop in our local supermarket! They are religious words, but they are words worth weighing. 'I have not come to call the righteous but sinners to repentance.'

Who are 'the righteous'? Righteousness is all about our relationship with the Holy God in whose hand is our existence. And 'the righteous' as Jesus is using it here, are those who assume – who sincerely believe that they themselves, and the lives they live are acceptable before God. The Pharisees, of course are the prime example with their meticulous keeping of the 613 commandments of God – as interpreted by themselves. But could it be us, as perhaps we sometimes look down on others, yet make the same assumption?

Who are 'sinners'? In modern usage it is those of whose way of life, of whose behaviour we disapprove. But that is very shallow. Who cares in modern society what my opinion is – or yours! But that is not how the Lord was using the word. He meant it in its true sense of missing the mark, like an arrow falling short of the target. He meant it of the precious people who he came to rescue. People who had fallen, or were falling, short of the Lord's God's calling to honour and obey him. Some more obviously, some more subtly. You won't like me for reminding you, but that is all of us. We, you and I, are falling short before the Lord God.

Sir James Simpson was an eminent 19th century professor of obstetrics and gynaecology in the University of Edinburgh and a pioneer of the use of anaesthetics. Towards the end of his illustrious career, he was asked by a reporter, "What was your most important discovery?" His quiet answer, "That I am a sinner and that the Lord Jesus Christ is my Saviour."

'I have not come to call the righteous but sinners to repentance.'
What is 'repentance'? Repentance is a change of heart, a change of thinking and a change of direction. It is not 'come and be religious' and be bound by our rules, regulations and ceremonial observances, as the scribes and Pharisees were teaching. But freely to turn and live for the Lord God in his world.

Repentance does mean leaving behind the things, the lifestyles, the patterns of behaviour that the Lord God has made clear are a stench in his nostrils. It does mean trusting, following and obeying the Lord Jesus with joyful obedience, as Matthew did. And it does mean, like Matthew, learning and coming to acknowledge who Jesus truly is – the Son of God, the King, who came not to be served, but to serve and to give his life a ransom for many – the King who came into this world to be the sacrificial Lamb of God, the Messiah, the anointed One – the King who will return at the end of the age in great power and glory as Lord and Judge of us all.

Matthew's meal was a meal with controversy, but a meal with a purpose.

Heavenly Father, have mercy upon us, enable us see through our natural self-righteous confidence, and so see how far short we are falling by our failure to honour and obey you with all our heart and mind and strength. Open our eyes to see our need of your mercy on us. Enable us to truly repent before you and believe on your beloved and anointed Son who loved us and gave himself for us, and so live freely and joyfully before you as your chosen, ransomed, forgiven sons and daughters.

Questions for personal reflection or discussion

1. Religion and religious observance, as an end in itself, can be a joyless thing. However, among the disciples, the ordinary people and the despised tax collectors and sinners – there was awe and

wonder and joy in the presence of the Lord Jesus, like the joy of a wedding. Do you know anything of each of these two scenes?

2. 'With their hearts full of sorrow, their hands full of work, and the world full of enmity and rage against them . . .' Is there a right time for great joy, and a right time to pray earnestly and to fast?

3. Matthew wanted to hear and learn more and he wanted others to meet and hear Jesus too. A great deal of good work for the Lord is done over a meal – as our circumstances permit. Can Matthew's example be a help and possibly a challenge to us?

4. The Pharisees, of course are the prime example of 'the righteous', with their meticulous keeping of the 613 commandments of God – as interpreted by themselves. But could it be us, as perhaps we sometimes look down on others, yet make the same assumption as they did?

5 "What was your most important discovery?" His quiet answer, "That I am a sinner and that the Lord Jesus Christ is my Saviour." Is that a discovery we understand and rejoice in?

6. In what ways does true repentance change the ways in which we live our daily lives?

Praying to the Father

Pray then like this: Our Father in heaven, hallowed be your name. Your kingdom come, your will be done, on earth as it is in heaven. Give us this day our daily bread, and forgive us our debts, as we also have forgiven our debtors. And lead us not into temptation, but deliver us from the evil one.

Matthew 6:9-13 English Standard Version

When they [Peter and John] were released, they went to their friends and reported what the chief priests and the elders had said to them. And when they heard it, they lifted up their voices together in prayer to God and said. "Sovereign Lord, who made the heaven and the earth and the sea, and everything in them . . ." And when they had prayed, the place in which they were gathered together was shaken, and they were all filled with the Holy Spirit and continued to speak the word of God with boldness.

Acts 4:23-24, 31 English Standard Version

Praying to the Father

It is not for me to interfere with the way you pray. But may I point you to the witness of God on the mount of transfiguration, 'This is my beloved Son, hear him,' that is, 'Do what he says'. And may I draw your attention to the witness of the writer to the Hebrews, 'In former times God spoke by the prophets, but in these last days he has spoken to us by his Son.'

For this reason, we should take very seriously what he, the Son of God, has said; what he has promised us, what he has warned us about, and what he has taught and commanded us to do. In the light of these things, may I point you to our Lord's teaching on prayer found in what we commonly call the 'Lord's Prayer'. In particular, may I point you to the wonderful invitation given to disciples to address our prayers to the Sovereign God, the Creator and King of the universe, and to address him as 'Our Father.'

Both Matthew and Luke record the Lord's Prayer. In Matthew's Gospel it is part of the Sermon on the Mount. In Luke's Gospel, it is Jesus' reply to the request of the disciples, "Lord, teach us to pray." The words vary a little but core of the prayer is essentially the same. Jesus said, 'When you pray, pray like this:' or as the King James' version puts it, 'pray after this manner,' 'Our Father in heaven . . .'

What a great privilege this invitation is! We are not taught to pray to a servant of God, no matter how eminent, but to the Sovereign Lord God himself; the One who has, in his hand, this world's very existence – your life and mine and all our circumstances. Disciples of the Lord Jesus, the Son of God, are invited to approach Almighty God as 'Abba,' 'Father,' my Father. We are offered the kind of relationship and freedom in prayer that a little child has with the most loving and caring of parents. We are given access by the Son of God to address the Lord God, his Father, as 'our Father.' (Romans 8:15 and 5:1-2) What a shame and what a loss if we choose to do something less!

If we choose not to pray directly to the Lord God himself, but feel we would do better to pray to some great man or woman of God to 'have a word on our behalf', we are choosing to put our own opinion over and above the way the Lord has taught us to pray. And of course, across the whole spectrum of human life, that is the essence of disobedience; doing what we choose to do, rather than what the Lord has commanded or taught us to do. The uncomfortable test of true faith is – obedience. Will we do as he has said, or will we choose not to?

Freedom in prayer
There is nothing rigid about being able to pray to our heavenly Father freely and informally as each situation demands. So we read in Acts chapter four that after the release of Peter and John by the religious leaders, the disciples and their fellow believers met and prayed spontaneously. They did not begin with the words, 'Our Father in heaven,' but with the words, 'Sovereign Lord . . .' Although the words are different, they follow the same basic principle of addressing our prayers to God our heavenly Father.

In and through the Lord Jesus, true disciples are given great freedom to come before Almighty God, the Sovereign Lord of the universe, in worship and in praise, and to plead with him freely.

In the prayer recorded in Acts chapter four, the disciples and believers were praying about a particular situation: the arrest of Peter and John, and then their subsequent release – on condition that Peter and John were 'not to speak or teach at all in the name of Jesus.' So, the disciples were praying with great relief and thanksgiving for their release, and they were praying for wisdom – in the light of the restrictions and threats – for holy boldness to continue unashamedly telling out the mighty works of God and proclaiming the gospel of the Lord Jesus.

The Lord heard their prayer, and with great boldness they continued, calling all who would hear, to repent before God of failure to honour and obey him, and to believe on his anointed Son, the One who laid down his life for our forgiveness, and whom God has appointed both Lord and Judge of us all.

The pattern of the Lord's Prayer itself

There is great freedom in speaking in prayer with our heavenly Father, but in the phrases of the Lord's Prayer, Jesus has given us a comprehensive prayer, and a wonderfully helpful basic pattern and framework for every situation.

It is not quite the gentle, sentimental wish list we tend to make it; 'May your name be honoured; may your kingdom come; may your will be done throughout the earth, as it is done in heaven . . . .' Rather, it is, or should be, a series of urgent cries from the heart.

In our land at present the Lord God is not honoured. As a nation, we have turned our back on God. By and large we ignore him and his holy ways, and his name is taken in vain; used as a swear-word, an expression of surprise or as a joke. 'Lord God, heavenly Father, cause your name to be held high, held in honour, feared and revered.'

'Father, cause your kingdom to come; all of us gladly and willingly living in submission to you, under your rule and governance, in accordance with your commandments and Fatherly instructions and those of your beloved and anointed Son, our Lord Jesus.' Only then will live in harmony with you, with one another and with this beautiful but hurting and spoiled planet in which you have set us.

'Cause your will to be done throughout the world in the way it is gladly and willingly done in heaven:' That is uncomfortable. It includes our behaviour in our own home, leisure and work setting. It includes our government's behaviour in the conduct of our national affairs, and our international affairs.

'Give us this day our daily bread.' Not caviar, but bread. All we really need to love you and serve you without fear or great anxiety – food and clothing, shelter and the harmonious support of one another.

'Forgive us . . . as we forgive others.' 'Please Lord, help me to constantly keep in mind your great mercy toward me, and to reflect that mercy to those around me – no matter how difficult or annoying I find them to be.' A truly Christian community will be marked out by the way the people genuinely care for one another and freely forgive one another.

'And lead us not into temptation.' Here is an acknowledgement that we can so easily be drawn away from the narrow path of true godliness.

'But deliver us from evil:' From evil thinking, evil speaking or evil deeds. From the evil one and those under the control of the evil one, be they human or spiritual influences. From being overwhelmed by an alien culture or godless regime.

Father, please awaken, stir up and revive your people the church to fulfil our calling to be your voice and ambassadors in this secular, godless age. For to you alone belongs all rule, power and glory.

Amen 'Yes. Lord God, may I add my cries to those of many others, bring these things about.'

Heavenly Father, hear our feeble prayers and like your first disciples – who were pressed hard by an unbelieving world – fill us afresh with your Holy Spirit and grant us boldness to proclaim your glorious name and gospel of grace.

Questions for personal reflection or discussion

1. Have you considered what a wonderful privilege it is to bring all our hopes, fears and longings before the One in whose hand is this world's existence, and address him as Father?
2. The great test of faith is not what we *say*, but what we *do*. Are we willing to trust and to obey the commandments and instructions of the Lord God and of his Son?
3. We can see from the disciples' freedom in prayer, that the Lord's Prayer is by no means a 'straight jacket'. But in what ways does it offer a guide to praying in all sorts of different situations?
4. Can you pick out phrases of the Lord's Prayer that particularly strike you as sharply touching this world's current challenges, or that have implications that touch your own life?

The Woman of Samaria

He [Jesus] left Judea and departed again for Galilee. And he had to pass through Samaria. So he came to a town in Samaria called Sychar, near the field that Jacob had given to his son Joseph. Jacob's well was there: so Jesus, wearied as he was from his journey, was sitting beside the well. It was about the sixth hour.

There came a woman of Samaria to draw water. Jesus said to her, "Give me a drink." (For his disciples had gone away into the city to buy food.) The Samarian woman said to him, "How is it that you, a Jew, ask for a drink from me, a woman of Samaria?" (For the Jews have no dealings with the Samaritans.) Jesus answered her, "If you knew the gift of God, and who it is that is saying to you, 'Give me a drink,' you would have asked him, and he would have given you living water." The woman said to him, "Sir, you have nothing to draw water with, and the well is deep. Where do you get that living water? Are you greater than our father Jacob? He gave us the well and drank from it himself, as did his sons and his livestock." Jesus said to her, "Everyone who drinks of this water will be thirsty again, but whoever drinks of the water that I will give him will never be thirsty again. The water that I will give him will become in him a spring of water welling up to eternal life." The woman said to him, "Sir, give me this water, so that I will not be thirsty or have to come here to draw water."

Jesus said to her, "Go, call your husband, and come here." The woman answered him, "I have no husband." Jesus said to her, "You are right in saying, 'I have no husband'; for you have had five husbands, and the one you now have is not your husband. What you have said is true." The woman said to him, "Sir, I perceive that you are a prophet. Our Fathers worshipped on this mountain, but you say that in Jerusalem is the place where people ought to worship." Jesus said to her, "Woman, believe me, the hour is coming when neither on this mountain nor in Jerusalem will you worship the Father. You worship what you do not know, we worship what we know, for salvation is from the Jews. But the hour is coming, and now is here, when the true worshippers will worship the Father in spirit and truth, for the Father is seeking such people to worship him. God is spirit and those who worship him must worship in spirit and truth." The woman said to him, "I know that Messiah is coming (he who is called Christ). When he comes, he will tell us all things." Jesus said to her, "I who speak to you am he."

Just then his disciples came back. They marvelled that he was taking to a woman, but no one said, "What do you seek?" or, "Why are you talking with her?" So the woman left her water jar and went away into the town and said to the people, "Come, see a man who told me all I ever did. Can this be the Christ?" They went out of the town and were coming to him . . .

Many Samaritans from that town believed in him because of the woman's testimony, "He told me all that I ever did." So when the Samaritans came to him, they asked him to stay with them, and he stayed there two days. And many more believed because of his word. They said to the woman, "It is no longer because of what you said that we believe, for we have heard for ourselves, and we know that this is indeed the Saviour of the world."

John 4:3-29 and 39-42 English Standard Version

The Samaritan Woman

Introduction

I am about to do something that is not wrong, but we just don't do it in the best of circles! I intend to introduce you to a lady of very doubtful character, a lady of somewhat ill repute, perhaps even a brazen hussy!

How dare I say that, and cast such a slur on the good lady's reputation? Surely she might have just been very sadly unfortunate. Her husbands might all have died of natural causes. The Pharisees put to Jesus the theoretical case of a virtuous woman who had lost all seven of her husbands.

We must not be hasty to be judgemental and condemn – the Lord did not do so. But if she was an entirely virtuous woman in such sad circumstances, the other women would have rallied round her to support her. She would have had no need to draw water alone at midday, the hottest part of the day, nor would she be likely to be currently living with a man who was not her husband.

When she told the people of Sychar about Jesus, she did not say, 'He told me all the sad things that have befallen me', but, 'He told me all that I ever did.'

You must judge for yourselves. Many spring to her defence and there is heated debate. However, the apostle John does not comment on her moral status as it is just a side issue.

The scene John describes

There were no cars or buses, and Jesus and the disciples were making their way from Judea to Galilee on foot, some 75 miles. Although strict Pharisees would take a longer route to avoid becoming 'defiled', the shortest route was to pass through Samaria.

Historically, Samaria was part of the area occupied by the ten tribes of Israel, many of whom were swept away into captivity by the Assyrians and replaced by people from across the Assyrian empire. In Jesus' time, it was occupied by people of mixed race. They also held a mixed faith, part Jewish, part added by Jeroboam as the kingdom was divided, and part imported from Assyria.

On Jesus' route was Jacob's well, the Greek says 'fountain' or 'spring' and it could well have been an underground fountain or spring as it was near the foot of Mount Gerizim. It was a long walk and we read that Jesus was tired and sat down at the well. 'He was wearied by the journey, so he sat down while the disciples went to buy food.'

The Lord Jesus was rightly called 'Emmanuel', God among us, both fully God and fully man, as the apostle Paul puts it, he was the Lord God in a human body There are many incidents throughout the gospels that display Jesus' divinity, but here is an incident that clearly displays his humanity. He was tired.

But this was clearly a 'divine appointment'. While Jesus was sitting by the well, a woman of Samaria came to draw water. The women would normally come to draw water much earlier in the day, when it was cooler, and they would come together. This woman came alone, and at mid day. Maybe, to avoid the criticism and the rebuff of the other women, she needed to come alone.

Jesus spoke to her. 'Religious' Jews would not speak to a Samaritan woman, and certainly would never drink from a Samaritan cup or vessel. But Jesus asked a favour, a drink, and so began the conversation. Jesus spoke to her of a spring of fresh water, 'living water'. She understood his offer literally, as it would save her the uncomfortably hot daily toil of collecting water and solve her difficulty of being shunned by the other women. But Jesus had something far greater in mind.

The Lord God 'looks on the heart'. Jesus was well aware of her circumstances. She had had five husbands and was now living with yet another man. Uncomfortable with the fact that Jesus knew this, she rapidly changed the subject to something safe, theoretical and theological. However, even that became challenging when she found herself confronted with God's Messiah.

Very soon after that, the disciples returned and it would have been impossible to have had such a conversation. It really was a divine appointment. When the disciples arrived, the woman left her water pot and went to tell the people of Sychar.

Why did the apostle John include this incident?
John was not writing for our entertainment or to introduce us to questionable ladies. At the conclusion of this gospel John writes, 'Now Jesus did many other signs . . .which are not written in this book; but these are written that you may believe that Jesus is the Christ [the Messiah], the Son of God, and that believing you might have life in his name.'

This conversation with the Samaritan woman is a significant part of the evidence John sets before us in order that we may have a secure and well-founded faith.

What would the apostle John have us learn from this incident? You can probably see more, but here are four things worth further prayerful thought:

Firstly – Living Water

Jesus would have given the Samaritan woman 'a spring of living water', if she had asked. We, too, need to ask for such a spring or fountain. It is the source and fountain spiritual life that the Lord God alone can put within us.

When Jesus speaks again of the 'living water' in John chapter 7, John adds 'Now this he said about the Spirit, which those who believed in him were to receive . . .' It is the Holy Spirit of God who opens our eyes to see the reality of the kingdom of heaven, and to see our desperate plight as human beings who daily fail to honour and to obey Almighty God. It is the Holy Spirit who enables us to truly turn from ungodly ways, seek the Lord God's face and find forgiveness in his Son. And from then on, the Lord God enlivens us, leads us and guides us by the Holy Spirit. It is indeed a God-given spring of living water springing up to eternal life. And it begins, as it continues, by humbly asking.

There is much encouragement in Scripture to ask. 'Open my eyes that I may behold wonderful things in your word.' 'You have not because you ask not.' 'Ask and it shall be given you, knock and it shall be opened to you, seek and you will find.' '. . . how much more will my heavenly Father give the Holy Spirit to those who ask.'

Secondly – Spiritual Discernment

The Samaritans accepted the first five books of the Old Testament, the books of Moses, but discarded the rest of the Old Testament; the writings, the psalms and the prophets, replacing its teachings with their own traditions. So there was much they did not know and much they had got wrong. As Jesus put it, 'You worship what you do not know.'

As our Lord urged the Samaritan woman, we, too, need to worship in spirit and in truth. And to be able to worship according to truth, rather than tradition, we need to be equipped by the Holy Spirit and by prayerfully reading the whole word of God. Otherwise we are in danger of embracing the traditions and wisdom of our age and culture. In particular, we need to take hold of the teaching of our Lord Jesus and his chosen apostles.

Thirdly – Spiritual Worship

The woman had been taught from her local pulpit to 'worship on this mountain'. But, 'worship in spirit and in truth' is not confined to places of worship, this mountain, that mountain, this church, chapel or cathedral. Or confined to the special rites and rituals that take place there; colour, candles, a solemn religious voice, or maybe drama, video clips and a stirring speaker.

To avoid the trap into which the woman had fallen, we need to be able to discern between 'religious activity' – and the true worship the Lord God seeks; a close and personal walk with and devotion to the Lord God our heavenly Father. The Lord Jesus is our pattern. His 'food and drink' was to do his Father's will, he was constantly in prayerful touch with his heavenly Father. Such a walk with the Lord is still a vital reality even in the isolation of prolonged illness and old age.

Fourthly – A firm grasp of who Jesus really is

'These are written that you may believe that Jesus is the Christ [the Messiah], the Son of God, and that believing you might have life in his name.'

The leading men of Sychar listened to the woman's testimony, 'He told me everything I ever did. Can he be the Messiah?' They did not dismiss it. They took note of it. But, on its own, it was not enough.

We, too, can gain only 'a nominal' or 'second hand faith' by what we hear from others. If it is only based on what we have been told, such a faith is not likely to prove a safe stronghold when facing the storms of life. It is likely to evaporate and let us down.

The people of Sychar did more than listen and take note of the woman's words. They came out and met Jesus, listened to him and spoke with him and asked him to stay a couple more days. He did, and as a result they became firmly convinced themselves of who he was. It was no longer a 'second hand' belief because she told them. They, themselves, were fully convinced that he was 'truly the anointed One of God, the Messiah, the Saviour of the world.'

Like the people of Sychar, we, too, have an active part to play; to come to him and spend time with him, listening and prayerfully reading the gospels for ourselves. Only as we do that will we be firmly and vitally convinced of who Jesus is, and rejoice in him; God's chosen and anointed One, the Messiah, the Son of God, our Lord and our Saviour.

Heavenly Father, thank you for the apostle John's record of this encounter. We pray that we may learn from it and become as fully convinced of your gospel truth as were the people of Sychar: settled and steadfast in knowledge and understanding, grounded in the person and work of yourself, of the Holy Spirit and of your Son the Lord Jesus Christ, the Saviour of the world.

Questions for personal reflection or discussion

1. Very soon after that, the disciples returned and it would have been impossible to have had such a conversation. It really was a divine appointment. Can you look back, reflect and pinpoint similar 'divine appointments'?

2. 'You would have asked him, and he would have given you living water.' There is much encouragement in Scripture to ask.

'Open my eyes that I may behold wonderful things in your word.' 'You have not because you ask not.' 'Ask and it shall be given you, knock and it shall be opened to you, seek and you will find.' '. . . how much more will my heavenly Father give the Holy Spirit to those who ask.' We readily ask for things like help with making decisions, or for healing for ourselves or others, but are we accustomed to asking for spiritual things Jesus described?

3. Are we in danger of embracing the traditions and wisdom of our age and culture? Do we need to take hold of the teaching of our Lord Jesus and his chosen apostles by reading the New Testament for ourselves?

4. The Lord Jesus is our pattern. His 'food and drink' was to do his Father's will, he was constantly in prayerful touch with his heavenly Father. Such a walk with the Lord is still a vital reality even in the isolation of prolonged illness and old age. Have you known aged and perhaps isolated Christian folk whose faith remains radiant and infectious?

5. It was no longer a 'second hand' belief because the woman told them. They, themselves, were fully convinced that Jesus was 'truly the anointed One of God, the Messiah, the Saviour of the world. How can we avoid a merely 'second hand' belief and be equally and personally fully convinced?

Zacchaeus

He [Jesus] entered Jericho and was passing through. And there was a man named Zacchaeus. He was a chief tax collector, and was rich. And he was seeking to see who Jesus was, but on account of the crowd he could not, because he was small of stature. So he ran on ahead and climbed up into a sycamore tree to see him, for he was about to pass that way. And when Jesus came to the place, he looked up and said to him, "Zacchaeus, hurry and come down; for I must stay at your house today." So he hurried and came down, and received him joyfully. And when they saw it, they all grumbled, "He has gone in to be the guest of a man who is a sinner." And Zacchaeus stood and said to the Lord, "Behold, Lord, half of my goods I give to the poor. And if I have defrauded any one of anything, I restore it fourfold." And Jesus said to him, "Today salvation has come to this house, since he also is a son of Abraham. For the Son of man came to seek and to save the lost."

Luke 19:1-10 English Standard Version

Zacchaeus

Many of us have known about Zacchaeus, the very little man who climbed a tree to see Jesus, since we were knee high to a grasshopper. But may I invite you to take another look? Maybe it will surprise you.

First some background.
Luke's Gospel, Chapter 18 tells of a rich young ruler who eagerly came to Jesus, but went away sorrowful because the cost of discipleship was too high. It tells us, too, of our Lord's words to the disciples, "How hard it is for a rich man to enter the kingdom of heaven." Yet here in Chapter 19 is a very rich man who clearly did enter the kingdom of heaven. With God, truly, all things are possible.

At the conclusion of the account of Zacchaeus we have our Lord saying, "For the Son of Man came to seek and to save the lost." The chapters following tell of the steep climb to Jerusalem, Gethsemane and the cross. It was for the lost, that the Son of God hung and suffered there. He gave his life to rescue, save and bring safely home to the Father those who by one means or another – like myself in my younger days – had strayed far from God and from godly ways. And who, like straying sheep, unless they are rescued, would ultimately perish.

Then Jericho. Jericho was on a main route to and from Jerusalem, well watered and surrounded by very fertile land. With taxes to collect on goods passing along that route and taxes to collect on the exports of the much prized locally grown dates and balsam, tax collectors could hardly help being wealthy.

And finally Zacchaeus. Zacchaeus was a tax collector for the Romans. Unsurprisingly, all such tax collectors were regarded as traitors and thieves. And Zacchaeus was a chief tax collector. The Greek describes him as the overseer or 'architect' of local tax collection. He was very rich. He wanted to see Jesus but was both short and hated. He could hardly expect to be offered a place at the front of a great crowd. Much more likely he would be nudged and elbowed to the back. Yet Zacchaeus was determined and resourceful, and he ran ahead and climbed a tree. Not our sycamore with its tall smooth trunk but more likely a wild fig or mulberry tree.

Jesus addressed him by name, giving Zacchaeus much more than a passing glimpse. Jesus said he must 'lodge', as the Greek has it, at his house. That was far more than a hated tax collector could have hoped for, and Zacchaeus welcomed him joyfully. And at some point, Zacchaeus spoke to Jesus of his giving to the poor and of his very generous restitution to anyone he had wronged.

It was after lodging with Zacchaeus that day, that the Lord Jesus declared that salvation, wholeness, restoration to the true family of God had come to that house.

Was it curiosity that drove Zacchaeus to climb the tree? All but one of the commentators believe it was. They see Zacchaeus as a rogue; a cheating, greedy, traitorous tax collector who had grown rich by his dishonesty. He had the privilege of spending time with Jesus and became a totally changed man. This is demonstrated by his turning his back on his past grasping ways and determining from now on to give away half of his income to the poor and to restore monies wrongly acquired. It is thought that Zacchaeus states this in the present tense, 'I give,' 'I restore,' to stress his determination to live a very different life from now on. By his encounter with the Lord Jesus, Zacchaeus was made a totally newly-created man; from grasping greed, to overflowing generosity. As Jesus declares, salvation came to his house and Zacchaeus became a true son of Abraham and child of God.

And, that is how it comes across in modern English translations of the Bible.

Those who have truly had an encounter with the Lord God and his Son our Lord Jesus will turn their back on any ungodly ways and become willing servants of God, living lives to the honour of the Lord God and his Son. If, like Zacchaeus, they are wealthy they may express their gratefulness to the Lord by using their wealth generously; becoming one of 'God's treasurers,' as the reformers put it.

However, does it worry you that Zacchaeus's statement is in the present tense, 'I give,' 'I restore,' rather than in the future tense, 'from now on I will give, I will restore'?

Does it worry you that his statement is so like the Pharisee's prayer in the temple, 'I fast twice a week, I give tithes of all that I get'?

If restoring money taken wrongly and giving money away made Zacchaeus a son of Abraham, that could be seen as earning or meriting God's favour by our human effort and lifestyle – exactly as the Pharisees were striving to do. But all our vain attempts to be good enough fall far short before him. They are not the Lord God's appointed way of salvation, but are, in Isaiah's words, 'as filthy rags'.

Finally, how did the Lord Jesus know Zacchaeus by name? And why did Jesus so determinedly go out of his way to spend time with him?

Taken together, these things cause me to ask, 'Is there is more than one way of understanding what was going on?'

Among the commentators, John Calvin alone writes that he believes that there is more to it than meets the eye. He asks, 'Had the Holy Spirit in some way prepared Zacchaeus and was this known to the Lord Jesus?'

May I invite you to consider how he might have done that?

Wealthy, well-watered Jericho lies at the foot of the mountainous road leading up to Jerusalem but, not far from Jericho, to the south and east is a vast dry expanse. The area is known as the wilderness. Standing at a height overlooking the wilderness, through the haze and dust you can see just a narrow, winding ribbon of green running through it; the valley of the river Jordan as it wends its way to the Dead Sea.

'Jordan,' 'Wilderness'. Do those ring a bell? 'The voice of one crying in the wilderness, "Prepare ye the way of the Lord ..."' Be ready for the Messiah's coming. Flee from the judgement to come. Repent. And great multitudes flocked to hear him and John baptized them in the river Jordan with a baptism of repentance, urging them 'to show fruits that befit repentance.'

Luke records, 'Tax collectors also came to him to be baptised, and he said to them, "Collect no more than is appointed you."'(Luke 3:12-13) In the light of that, could it be that the Lord God had already begun a work in Zacchaeus's life? Touched by God under the ministry of John the Baptist, could Zacchaeus have truly repented; turned from past thieving ways, and been eagerly awaiting the coming of the Messiah? Here was a tax collector with a difference. He would still be a despised tax collector, 'a sinner,' – one living a disgraceful and scandalous life, as the crowd saw him and stereotyped all tax collectors to be – but here was a tax collector of godly integrity.

If so, it would explain why the Romans had made him a chief tax collector. Just as the pagan authorities had earlier recognised Joseph and Daniel to be men of integrity who could be trusted, could the Romans have recognised Zacchaeus as one who would efficiently and honestly collect deliver the taxes they required?

It would also explain Zacchaeus's eager determination to see this person who was causing such a stir. Could he be the One of whom John had spoken? Could he be the One who was to come, the Messiah? Rich men of status do not climb trees! But Zacchaeus cared nothing for dignity, he knew he *must* to see Jesus.

It would also explain why Jesus addressed him by name. Zacchaeus could never have invited Jesus to his house. Rabbis and religious leaders never came anywhere near tax collectors. There would be no chance. But Jesus invited himself. "Zacchaeus hurry and come down for; I must stay at your house today." 'You have not chosen me, but I have chosen you.' It was a divine appointment. It was more than Zacchaeus could ever have hoped for. Is that is why Zacchaeus climbed down with haste and received Jesus joyfully?

The scribes and Pharisees did not 'receive Jesus joyfully' but here is one of that despised group, a tax collector, who did. 'He came to his own people and they received him not, but to those who received him he gave the right, the power, the authority, to become the sons and daughters of God.'

Could it be that Zacchaeus had repented under the ministry of John the Baptist, and now receiving Jesus, believed? Salvation came to his house.

I have come to believe that Zacchaeus was called and chosen. God had had mercy on him, and had caused him to repent of the normal fraudulent ways of tax collectors, and had caused him to be eagerly awaiting the Messiah. The Lord Jesus, coming by this route to Jerusalem, came out of his way to 'bother' and spend time with Zacchaeus. Zacchaeus received him joyfully and believed.

And Jesus said to him, "Today salvation has come to this house, since he also is a son of Abraham. For the Son of man came to seek and to save the lost." The gospel call is to repent and believe. Zacchaeus had truly repented under the ministry of John the Baptist, and now, receiving Jesus joyfully, believed. And that is the God's chosen way of salvation. It is how we become the true sons and daughters of God.

Heavenly Father, we thank you for this account of your Son's troubling with the tax collector, Zacchaeus. By your Holy Spirit lead us to truly repent and to believe on your Son, our Lord Jesus. And on behalf of those of us who, like Zacchaeus, know ourselves to be sinners saved by grace, like him, we stand amazed that you bothered with us.

Questions for personal reflection or discussion

1. Zacchaeus was made a totally newly-created man; from grasping greed, to overflowing generosity. In what ways does that demonstrate true repentance?

2. How might such true repentance touch our lives? For example lifestyle choices and lifetime habits of greed, selfishness, arrogance, grumbling, criticism, gossip?

3. Those who have truly had an encounter with the Lord God and his Son our Lord Jesus will turn their back on any ungodly ways and become willing servants of God, living lives to the hon-

our of the Lord God and his Son. In what ways can we help and encourage on another to do this?

4. Do we personally stand back amazed that the Lord God and his Son bothered with us?

5. 'Had the Holy Spirit in some way prepared Zacchaeus?' Looking back over life can you see the hand of the Lord God, by his Holy Spirit, leading, guiding, preparing you?

References

The voice of one crying in the wilderness, "Prepare ye the way of the Lord ..." – Luke 3:4 quoted from Isaiah 40:3

Collect no more than is appointed you. – Luke 3:12-13

You have not chosen me, but I have chosen you – John 15:16

He came to his own, and his own people did not receive him. But to all who did receive him, who believed on his name, he gave the right to become the children of God. – John 1:11-12

As filthy rags – Isaiah 64:6

She has done what she could

It was now two days before the Passover and the Feast of Unleavened Bread. And the chief priests and the scribes were seeking how to arrest him (Jesus) by stealth, and kill him. For they said, "Not during the feast, lest there be an uproar of the people."

And while he was at Bethany in the house of Simon the leper, as he was reclining at table, a woman came with an alabaster flask of ointment of pure nard, very costly, and she broke the flask and poured it over his head. There were some who said to themselves indignantly, "Why was the ointment wasted like that? For this ointment could have been sold for more than three hundred denarii and given to the poor." And they scolded her. But Jesus said, "Leave her alone. Why do you trouble her? She has done a beautiful thing to me. For you always have the poor with you, and whenever you want, you can do good for them. But you will not always have me. She has done what she could; she has anointed my body beforehand for burial. And truly, I say to you, wherever the gospel is proclaimed in the whole world, what she has done will be told in memory of her."

Then Judas Iscariot, who was one of the twelve, went to the chief priests in order to betray him to them. And when they heard it, they were glad and promised to give him money. And he sought an opportunity to betray him.

Mark 14:1-11 English Standard Version

She has done what she could

The incident of this woman breaking open a sealed and very valuable flask of ointment and pouring the ointment over Jesus is recorded in the gospels of Matthew, Mark and John. It took place just a few days before Jesus' arrest and crucifixion.

May I invite you to look at the setting, the woman and her gift, the disciples' reaction to such generosity, and Jesus' defence and commendation of her?

The setting
In the gospel record, this incident is sandwiched between the account of the chief priests' and scribes' determination to arrest and kill Jesus, and Judas' offer to betray Jesus to them for money.

Mark tells us that the meal took place in the home of a man known as Simon the leper. In all probability a man healed of his leprosy by Jesus. (If he had not been healed, he could never invite other people to his house. And if he had been healed, his gratefulness would be unbounded.)

Mathew's account is very similar, both emphasise the ointment's great value, Matthew comments that it was 'an alabaster flask of very expensive ointment'. This detail is helpful as it suggests that this carved stone flask of ointment was an almost priceless import from India, and likely to be the most valuable possession in the home.

John's account of this incident notes that the meal took place in Bethany, but he does not specify in whose house. He records that the meal was served by Martha and Mary and their brother Lazarus. Lazarus was present at the table. John also records that it was Mary who broke open the flask of ointment in honour of Jesus.

The woman

Meals were very open affairs, and Mark simply tells us that 'a woman came'. Matthew records that 'a woman came up to him'. John tells us that the woman was Mary, whose brother Lazarus Jesus had raised from the dead. Mary shows her deep and heartfelt gratitude by the extravagance of her gift. She broke open this very valuable alabaster flask of perfume. Unopened, it would have been worth almost a year's wages for a working man. Yet Mary broke it open. And that, not to offer a few drops to an honoured guest, but to lavishly shower him with it, head, feet body. This was an expression of unrestrained gratitude and love.

It may have been even more than that, for it was Mary who sat at Jesus' feet and listened carefully to him when he had earlier spent time in their home (Luke 10:38-42). Mary may have been more open and aware than the disciples of Jesus' words concerning his arrest and his being put to death.

The disciples held fast to the idea of an earthly kingdom and their own honoured positions in it, and so had no ears to hear or accept what Jesus said about his suffering and death. But Mary listened to his every word, and may have been aware that this could be her last and only opportunity to show her great love and gratitude.

The disciples' reaction

'What a waste. The unopened flask should have been sold and the money given for relief of the poor. It could have been sold for almost a year's earnings for a working man.' Mark simply records the disciples grumbling. John tells us that the grumbling was primarily Judas. Judas was the disciple who looked after the money and would have been well aware of the great value of this ointment.

Perhaps, too, he was painfully aware of this lost opportunity to lay his hands on such wealth. John tells us that Judas was not averse to helping himself from the disciples' common purse. (John 12:4-7)

Did this lost opportunity to secure a very valuable flask and sell it for money, provoke him to seize another opportunity? Very soon after this incident, we are told, Judas went to the chief priests and offered to betray Jesus to them – and was promised money if he did so.

The Reformers were constantly challenging their hearers to 'guard their hearts'. The craving desire for wealth is certainly one of the areas to watch very carefully.

The Lord's response to the grumbles
But Jesus said, "Leave her alone. Why do you trouble her? She has done a beautiful thing to me. For you always have the poor with you, and whenever you want, you can do good for them. But you will not always have me. She has done what she could; she has anointed my body beforehand for burial."

Here lies the challenge of the incident. The woman, Mary, did what she could, while she could, and she did it for the Lord Jesus. That is a most useful and helpful pattern for our own use of time and money and opportunity.

Mary had in her possession this most precious ointment or perfume. Here was her opportunity to use it, and to use it well. The gospel challenge is the same for us, as we have opportunity, no matter at what personal expense, to do what we can.

Mary saw and took her fleeting opportunity to honour the Master. A few days later it would have been too late. Jesus would have been arrested and the process leading to his crucifixion begun. The challenge of the incident for us is to recognise that if we do not grasp the opportunity given to us to honour our Lord, the opportunity will pass. It will be too late.

Mary did what she did out of love and gratitude to Jesus for what he had done. That same motive, or lack of it, will plumb the depths of our own hearts and tell us whether we have really grasped the wonder of the Lord God's mercy and love towards us, fallen as we are, as we see it at Calvary's cross. 'It was for us he hung and suffered there. . .' 'In my place condemned he stood, sealed my pardon with his blood.' Or in the words of a godly saint, who thought as Mary did, "He has done that for me, there is nothing I would not do for him".

The disciples, and Judas in particular, had no understanding of such love, gratitude and devotion. Nor did they have Mary's spiritual insight, or realise the significance of what she had done until very much later. That they did come to see it and treasure it, is evident from the fact that Matthew, Mark and John all record what she did, and so fulfil the Lord's prophecy that her action would be told, in her honour and memory, all over the world, wherever the gospel is preached.

Conclusion
Our heavenly Father constantly invites us to pray, but does not ask of us things that our situation or circumstances make impossible. However, we sometimes fret fruitlessly about the things we would do 'if we could'. For example, we may long to: 'Stop the fighting in . . .' 'Change the thinking of politicians.' 'Replace humanistic church leaders with truly God-fearing ones.' 'Halt the slide of our generation into atheistic ways of thinking and behaviour, and turn the nation back to God.' Nevertheless, be it small, or very signifi-

cant, with prayer and the Lord's enabling we must do what we can, while we can, and do it for his honour.

Heavenly Father, grant us the humility to learn from this brief account to have open ears to the teaching of your word and the promptings of the Holy Spirit, and so learn to grasp the windows of opportunity you give us to do what we can, while we can, for the honour of yourself and of your Son, our Lord Jesus.

Questions for personal reflection or discussion

1. 'As we have opportunity, no matter at what personal expense, to do what we can.' That is quite challenging, have we reflected on what part we can play to bring honour to our Lord?

2. 'A few days later it would have been too late.' With hindsight, can we see things we could have done? Can this incident help us to see the fleeting nature of our opportunities and spur us to grasp them while we can?

3. 'Mary did what she did out of love and gratitude to Jesus for what he had done. That same motive, or lack of it, will plumb the depths of our own hearts.' Is that a rather uncomfortable thought?

4. 'Mary did what she could, while she could, and she did it for the Lord Jesus.' How useful and helpful a pattern is that for our own use of our possessions, our time, our money and our opportunities?

5a. Our heavenly Father constantly invites us to pray, but does not ask of us things that our situation or circumstances make impossible. However, do we sometimes fret fruitlessly about the things we would do 'if we could'?

5b. Should we wring our hands in helpless despair, or, be it small or very significant, with prayer and the Lord's enabling, do what we can, while we can, and do it for his honour?

Hymns quoted

'It was for us he hung and suffered there. . .' A line from *There is a green hill far away* by Cecil Frances Alexander

'In my place condemned he stood, sealed my pardon with his blood.' A line from *"Man of Sorrows!" what a name* by Philipp Bliss

Footnote

For our encouragement, William Wilberforce, 'did what he could' in his generation. As a member of Parliament, he stood almost alone against the thinking, and the practice of the world of his day. He also stood against the vested interest of many of his fellow members of Parliament. But under the hand of God, and with the prayers and support of his fellow Christians, he is famous for eventually securing the abolition of slavery.

The Triumphal Entry into Jerusalem

And when [Jesus] had said these things, he went on ahead, going up to Jerusalem. When he drew near to Bethphage and Bethany at the mount called Olivet, he sent two of his disciples, saying, "Go into the village in front of you, where on entering you will find a colt tied, on which no-one has yet sat. Untie it and bring it here. If anyone asks you, 'Why are you untying it?' you shall say this: 'The Lord has need of it.'"

So those who were sent went and found it just as he had told them. And as they were untying the colt, its owners said to them, "Why are you untying the colt?" And they said, "The Lord has need of it." And they brought it to Jesus, and throwing their cloaks over the colt, they set Jesus on it. And as he rode along, they spread their cloaks on the road.

As he was drawing near – already on the way down the Mount of Olives – the whole multitude of his disciples began to rejoice and praise God with a loud voice for all the mighty works they had seen, saying, "Blessed is the king who comes in the name of the Lord!" "Peace in heaven and glory in the highest!"

And some of the Pharisees in the crowd said to him, "Teacher, rebuke your disciples!" He answered, "I tell you, if these were silent the very stones will cry out."

And when he drew near and saw the city, he wept over it, saying, "Would that you, even you, had known on this day the things that make for peace! But now they are hidden from your eyes. For the days will come upon you when your enemies will set up a barricade round you, and surround you and hem you in on every side, and tear you to down the ground, you and the children within you. And they will not leave one stone upon another, because you did not know the time of your visitation."

Luke 19:28-44 English Standard Version

The Triumphal Entry

The setting and then the event itself
We tend to consider the triumphal entry of our Lord into Jerusalem, riding on a donkey and accompanied by great crowds, as an isolated event. But it is not, it is the conclusion of a long journey on foot of nearly 100 miles. Luke spends ten chapters of his Gospel recording it, chapters that include some of the best known parables such as the great banquet, the lost sheep, the lost coin and the prodigal son.

Way back in chapter 9 verse 51, we read, 'When the days drew near for him to be received up, he set his face to go to Jerusalem.' And then, over many chapters, Luke records that long journey walking from village to village, town to town preaching and teaching. In chapter 13 verse 22 we read, 'He went on his way through towns and villages, teaching and journeying towards Jerusalem.'

In verse 31 of chapter 13, Jesus was warned not to go to Jerusalem. And his response? "O Jerusalem, Jerusalem, killing the prophets and stoning those who are sent to you! How often would I have gathered your children together as a hen gathers her brood under her wings, and you would not! Behold, your house is forsaken. And I tell you, you will not see my face until you say, 'Blessed is he who comes in the name of the Lord!' (which the great crowd of ordinary people did at the triumphal entry, and which may have a far greater fulfilment when Jesus returns.)

Words to ponder
Before we continue following Jesus' journey, may I draw your attention to some of the most solemn and terrifying words in Scripture? They explain why Jesus wept over Jerusalem, and in various forms occur again and again throughout the Bible. The words are, 'and you would not', or 'you were not willing'. It seems that the Sovereign Lord God respects our wilful decisions and 'gives us up', or 'gives us over', to the terrifying consequences of them.

For example, Isaiah urging the people to trust the Lord God in the face of Babylonian aggression, says, 'In quietness and confidence shall be your strength'; quietness before God and confidence in God. But you said, "No!" And the people of Israel were swept into captivity. (Isaiah 39:15)

Jeremiah, setting out the whole purpose and calling of God's ancient covenant people, writes, '. . . I made the whole house of Israel and the whole house of Judah cling to me, declares the Lord, that they might be for me a people, a name, a praise, and a glory, but they would not listen.' (Jeremiah 13:11)

At the dedication of Solomon's temple, the Lord God gave a promise that stands forever and is highly relevant today. '. . . if my people who are called by my name humble themselves, and pray and seek my face and turn from their wicked ways [ungodly ways], then I will hear from heaven and will forgive their sin and heal their land'. (2 Chronicles 7:14) May I ask, when did you last hear of a call by Jewish leader to his fellow Jewish people to humble themselves before God, turn from their self-confident, atheistic ways and pray?

And here, these words of Jesus, 'How often would I have gathered . . . but you would not!' And in A.D. 70, Jerusalem was taken by the Romans, the temple burned down and the people either slain or taken into slavery.

That is all ancient history, you may say. But I have to confess that the words very sharply apply to me. I knew full well that the Lord God would have me become a Christian minister, but for ten years, 'I would not hear', 'I was not willing', 'I would not'.

Or supposing for a moment we apply those words to the Bible's most famous verse, 'God so loved the world that he gave his one and only Son, that whoever believes in him will not perish but have eternal life.' 'But you would not!' How solemn and terrifying the words then become. God so loved the world – that is you and me, your and my family members; brothers and sisters, sons and daughters, children and grandchildren. '. . . gave his only Son that those who believe in him . . .' 'But you would not!' 'You were not willing!' 'You would not listen.'

That is our modern society. That is us. Solemn and terrifying words. Words worth pondering. 'But you would not!' 'You were not willing!'

But, lest you are not sure you want to continue reading . . .

Continuing the journey to Jerusalem
In chapter 17, Luke again picks up the journey, in verse 11 we read, 'On the way to Jerusalem he was passing along between Samaria and Galilee. And as he entered a village he was met by ten lepers, who stood at a distance and lifted up their voices saying, "Jesus, Master, have mercy on us."'

And finally in chapter 19, Luke describes the last but one part of the journey. In Jericho, Jesus had just taught the parable of the pounds or minas. Reading from verse 28, 'And when he has said these things, he went on ahead, going up to Jerusalem.' 'Going up' is a slight understatement. Jericho is approximately 800 feet below sea level and Jerusalem is approximately 2,500 feet above it, and the climb is through some very rough and notoriously bandit infested terrain. Jesus climbed that steep road and came to Bethphage and Bethany, the villages on the Mount of Olives overlooking Jerusalem.

Israel's true King

And now there is a very great change. Whereas throughout his ministry Jesus had silenced those who recognised him to be the 'Son of God', 'the Holy One of God', the 'Son of David', Israel's true King. Jesus now makes the truth of these titles plain and public by this very dramatic act of the triumphal entry into Jerusalem.

Jesus had to keep it secret until now, or it would have been greatly misunderstood. The people, led by the scribes and Pharisees, were longing and looking for a military Messiah who would throw out the Roman conquerors and restore Israel, as a nation, to the glory days of Kings David and Solomon.

But, now it can be plainly seen that this is not his calling or purpose, Jesus declares he is Israel's true King and Messiah, very publicly accepting the titles, prayers and praises of the crowd. 'Blessed is the King who comes in the name of the Lord!'

The triumphal entry completed Jesus' long journey to Jerusalem. It was also the fulfilment of Scripture. Long before, Zechariah had prophesied (Ch. 9 verse 9) 'Rejoice . . . shout, O daughter of

Jerusalem! Lo, your king comes to you; just and triumphant is he, humble and riding on an ass, on a colt the foal of an ass.'

Publicly Jesus rode into Jerusalem. It was a triumphal entry, not on a war horse, not surrounded by great army, not dragging captives in chains – but in humility and in peace, on a beast of peace, freely accompanied by a great crowd of ordinary people proclaiming things like, 'Blessed is he who comes in the name of the Lord!' 'Hosanna to the Son of David!'

What was the Pharisees' reaction? They recognised what was going on and hated every moment of it. They had eyes to see and ears to hear all the evidence that had been set before them during Jesus' ministry – his words, his miracles, the frequent fulfilment of their own Scriptures, 'but they would not', they 'were not willing' to accept or to acknowledge who he truly was. Hence, 'Silence the people!' 'Rebuke them!' 'Stop them!' But if he had, the very stones would have cried out and declared the truth the people were shouting.

The king who came in the name of the Lord – and yet . . .
And when he drew near and saw the city he wept over it, saying, "Would that you, even you, had known on this day the things that make for peace! But now they are hidden from your eyes . . . And they will not leave one stone upon another in you, because you did not know the time of your visitation." (Luke 19, verse 41-44)

Jesus came to Jerusalem as Israel's rightful King and Redeemer – but 'they would not,' 'they were not willing'. In AD 70 the Romans reduced Jerusalem and the temple within it to rubble. No wonder that Jesus wept over the city and the suffering of the ordinary people within it.

Finally, for ourselves, personally
When the Lord God by his Holy Spirit stirs us and challenges us to submit, to bow the knee, to confess our failing before Almighty God, and to gratefully welcome his Son as our Redeemer and King, or to undertake some calling or task on his behalf, by the mercy of God, may it not be said of us, 'but you would not', 'you were not willing.'

Heavenly Father, open our eyes to see the 'things that make for peace' – who Jesus truly is: King of kings and Lord of lords, Emmanuel, God among us, and what he has done for us as the Lord God's appointed Redeemer who loved us and gave himself for us. By your grace, enable us to live grateful, faithful and obedient lives before you.

Questions for personal reflection or discussion

1. Why did Jesus weep over Jerusalem? Was it the future destruction of the magnificent buildings, or was it for some other reason?

2. Would he have cause to weep over our modern cities?

3. Would Jesus have cause to weep over many of those leading our modern denominational churches?

4. Why did the religious leaders in Jerusalem, the centre of Jewish worship, consistently ignore, refuse to hear, reject and suppress and even kill the messengers of God? They did so from the prophets, to John the Baptist, to our Lord himself, and then onwards, as they stoned Stephen and attempted to silence Peter and John.

5. Why is it so often the case that it is 'the religious' people who are most resistant to New Testament belief, and to believers?

6. Are we aware of times in our own life when 'we would not listen', 'we were not willing', 'we would not'?

Encounter with Pilate

From then on, Pilate sought to release [Jesus], but the Jews cried out, "If you release this man, you are not Caesar's friend. Everyone who makes himself a king opposes Caesar." So when Pilate heard these words, he brought Jesus out and sat down on the judgement seat at a place known as The Stone Pavement, and in Aramaic Gabbatha. Now it was the day of Preparation of the Passover. It was about the sixth hour. He said to the Jews, "Behold you King!" They cried out, "Away with him, away with him, crucify him!" Pilate said to them, "Shall I crucify your King?" The chief priests answered, "We have no king but Caesar." So he delivered him over to them to be crucified.

John 19:12-16 English Standard Version

Jesus brought before Pilate

First, some background
Jesus' trial before Pilate is recorded in each of the four gospel accounts. Together, they give us increasing insights into the encounter.

The passage at the top of the page is a small section of John's account. Matthew records that Caiaphas, the high priest, had put Jesus on oath, "I adjure you by the living God, tell us if you are the Christ, the Son of God." Matthew 26:63. Jesus did not deny it, he affirmed that it was as the high priest had said. For that reply, the Jewish religious leaders condemned Jesus to death for blasphemy.

Under their Roman conquerors the religious leaders could condemn a man but could not put him to death by crucifixion. That penalty was reserved to the Romans, so the chief priests had no option but to bring Jesus before the Roman Procurator or Governor, Pontius Pilate.

The encounter from Pilate's point of view
Pontius Pilate was the most powerful man in Judea. He lived in grand style in the Roman fortress or palace surrounded by servants. A position many would envy. He was a very exalted and powerful man. Appointed by Tiberius Caesar he had all the power and might of the Roman conquerors at his disposal, and had a section of the Roman army under his command. Pilate had the life, or the death, of all Caesar's subject people in Judea in his hand.

Pilate did not condemn Jesus, but did allow the forceful demands of the chief priests to prevail. Despite his own better judgement, he was the man who handed over Jesus to be crucified.

Unsurprisingly, Pilate has a very bad press, he is widely condemned as being weak, yet personally I have great sympathy for him. His was an exalted post, yet, great honour as it was, it carried great difficulties. Pilate was constantly accountable for his decisions and actions to Caesar, and he was well aware that Tiberius prided himself in well governed provinces.

The Jewish people were a notoriously strong-willed and difficult people to rule and bring into quiet subjection to their Roman overlords. The wily Jewish leaders could always undermine Pilate by arranging a bad report of him to reach Caesar's ears; some seeming failure to strengthen Caesar's hold on the people, or apparent failure to keep down a rebel leader. This was the trump card the chief priests held and, as in Jesus' case, used to 'persuade' the Roman governor to do as they wished. So they said to Pilate 'If you let this man live you are not Caesar's friend.' Word will get back to Caesar that you are disloyal to him, you have released a traitor against him.

Again, should Pilate fail to quell a potential riot, such as the one the Jewish leaders began to stir up when Pilate would have released Jesus, such a failure would also undermine his standing as Governor before Caesar.

By one technique or another, the chief priests had Pilate, technically powerful as he was, 'tied up', or as we might say 'buttoned up'. He could not win.

Pilate was a perceptive man, and ruthless as he had to be on some occasions to exert Roman authority, he could see that Jesus was an innocent man. He had not committed any crime. It was out of malice and envy the Jewish leaders would have him put to death. Pilate sincerely wanted to do what he clearly saw was right, an understanding only confirmed by his wife's message. "Have nothing to do with that righteous man, for I have suffered much because of him today in a dream." (Matthew 27:19) What was he to do?

We read in the gospel accounts that Pilate was even more afraid when he heard that the Jewish leaders had condemned Jesus for claiming to be the Son of God. Was he, Pilate, in some way handling a case involving 'the gods'? Pilate had a fearful awareness of the greatness, the weight, the significance of the decision that rested on his shoulder, but the buck stopped with him, he had to make the judgement.

Pilate's was not a comfortable situation. If you were in his position, what would you do? If he released Jesus, as he wanted to do and knew he ought to do, an evil report of his apparent disloyalty would reach Caesar's ears. If he failed to quell the riot, that would again reflect very badly on the effectiveness of his governorship.

He would be reported as being 'inadequate' to Caesar. That would mean the end of his career and possibly of his life.

In the face of the cunning, demanding, shouting Jewish leaders and a brewing riot, Pilate did the only thing he believed he could. He declared Jesus innocent, washed his hands of the affair, and handed Jesus over to the will of the Jewish religious leaders – to have him put him to death. (Matthew 27:24-26)

The encounter from Jesus' point of view

We have looked at the encounter from Pilate's perspective. Now we must look at it from our Lord's. Why did he say so little to Pilate? Jesus was not taken by surprise by his arrest and false trial. He was not overtaken or overwhelmed by fast moving circumstances. Three times he had said to the disciples that he would be arrested, treated shamefully, and put to death. He came to do his Father's will. 'The Son of Man came not to be served but to serve and to give his life a ransom for many' (Mark 10:45). He had left the glory of heaven to lay down his life for his sheep, his people. The cross lay at the heart of the purposes of God.

Under the hand of the Lord God, Jesus' encounter with Pilate the Roman Governor was a part of the final scene in the purposes of God. He did not need to respond to the string of false charges of the chief priests. He was innocent with regard to any crime. He was no threat to Rome, his kingdom was 'not of this world'. Even at this point he could have been delivered by an army of heaven's angels, but that was not his desire, or his Father's will, so Jesus said very little, as the prophet Isaiah had said, '. . . he opened not his mouth.'

The power of Rome, the strangle-hold of the religious leaders, and the almighty power of God
There are some very significant words recorded in John 19:10-13.

'Pilate therefore said to him, "Do you refuse to speak to me? Do you not know that I have power to release you, and power to crucify you?" Jesus answered him, "You would have no power over me unless it had been given you from above; therefore the one who handed me over to you is guilty of a greater sin." From then on Pilate tried to release him, but the Jews cried out, "If you release this man, you are no friend of Caesar. Everyone who claims to be a king sets himself against Caesar". When Pilate heard these words, he brought Jesus outside and sat on the judge's bench . . .'

Who was responsible for delivering our Lord to Pilate? Judas was Satan's dupe who for money arranged Jesus' arrest, but it was the religious leaders under Caiaphas, the High Priest, who 'tried' him with a mock trial, falsely accused him and delivered him to Pilate to ratify their decision to have him put to death.

Beneath the surface you have here a confrontation. Pilate – who had all the power of the Roman conquerors. The Jewish religious leaders – who had power over Pilate. However, the Lord Jesus, the Son of God, is the One to whom has been given all power and authority. In this encounter, the might and power of Rome, and the angry voices of the religious leaders, came face to face with the power of Almighty God; the God in whose hand is our very existence, and all our circumstances. What a confrontation! Both Pilate and his wife had something of an awareness of these things.

Why then was Jesus silent? Why did he not fight? Or at least put to flight the Jewish leaders and sweep away the power of Rome? As he said, he could have done. Our Lord chose not to. The whole purpose of the life and of the death of the Lord Jesus, was to fulfil his Father's great purpose. With unerring power, the Lord God was working his purpose out.

And what was that purpose? The provision of an amnesty, a way of forgiveness, an atoning sacrifice for all those who would humble themselves before the Lord God, and pray, and turn from ungodly ways, and believe on his chosen and anointed Son. As the apostle John puts it, 'God so loved the world that he gave his only Son, that those who believe on him might not perish, [be swept away by the just judgement of God as being his disobedient and rebellious subjects,] but have everlasting and eternal life' – life that not even death can snatch away. (John 3:16)

Heavenly Father, This clash of power is set before us by all four gospel writers, not just for our interest, but for our learning. By your grace help each one of us to understand and take hold of your great purposes in your Son and his laying down of his life. Enable us to humble ourselves and accept that 'it was for us he hung and suffered there' and so live a life of deep gratitude, and of humble obedience.

Questions for personal reflection or discussion

1. Would you condemn Pilate as a weak and ineffectual Governor?
2. In what ways did the religious leaders have Pilate under their control?
3. Would it be comfortable to find yourself ground between the upper millstone of Caesar's rule, and the lower millstone of very clever, very wily Jewish leaders?

4. Seeing that it was out of envy that the religious leaders wanted Jesus crucified, what would you have done had you been in Pilate's position?

5. Beneath the surface of angry shouts and cunning, can you see the over-ruling hand of the Lord God? (After the resurrection, the disciples certainly came to see the trial in this light, Acts 4:27-28.)

6. What part did the trial before Pilate play in the overall purposes of The Lord God?

Footnote

The name 'Pontius' is not generally thought to be a title indicating the he was called to be a 'bridge builder' between Caesar and his conquered people, but thought to be his family name, like our surnames, indicating that he came from the clan of Pontii.

Aspects of the Cross

New Testament Reflections on the Cross

What gives the cross of Christ its unique significance?
The Romans used crucifixion widely to shame and to deter would be rebels, robbers and runaway slaves, and as the ultimate way of subduing conquered peoples. It was not unusual to see a group of soldiers leading away a man with a cross. Being hung on a cross was such a slow, agonizing and shameful death that Roman citizens were not allowed to be crucified.

Among so many, in what way was the crucifixion of Jesus different? Some people focus on the agony of the cross – the anguish and the horror of all he suffered for us. However, there have been many other agonizing deaths. There were two others who suffered in the same way on either side of Jesus on that day.

The significance of the cross of the Lord Jesus does not lie in the human agony, but in who it was who was crucified. Jesus was not just a 'religious leader' or a 'great prophet'. He was great David's greater Son, the Messiah, the Christ, Emmanuel, God among us in a human body. When we come to recognise that, there is a new and unfathomable depth to the agony of that particular cross. For what was being accomplished on that cross involved the temporary tearing apart of the bond of love and unity between God the Father and God the Son. Hence the terrible cry of Jesus from the cross, 'My God, my God, why have you forsaken me?' – a quotation from Psalm 22.

Was Jesus swept to his death?
Was Jesus' death the inevitable consequence of the accumulation of the hatred of the scribes and Pharisees, the treachery of Judas, the anger of the potentially riotous crowd shouting, 'Crucify him!'? Did these things build up into a kind of tidal wave that swept him to his death? From a human point of view, there have been many who thought so.

However, the apostles and those who joined them in writing the books of the New Testament, came to see these as the human instruments fulfilling the purposes of God.

From the moment the Lord God gave Peter an understanding of who Jesus truly was, Jesus began to teach his disciples that he would be arrested, spitefully treated and put to death. (Mark 8:27-32, 9: 30-32, 10:32-34) Jesus spoke of 'necessity being laid on him', of 'being constrained until it was accomplished'. In the garden of Gethsemane we read of Jesus sweating great tears as of blood, 'Father if this cup may pass – nevertheless your will be done.'

After the resurrection, Luke records Jesus explaining to two disciples that it was 'necessary that the Christ should suffer these things . . .' And he records the disciples acknowledging this, '. . . for truly in this city there were gathered together against your holy servant Jesus, whom you anointed, both Herod and Pontius Pilate, along with the Gentiles and the peoples of Israel, to do whatever your hand and your plan had predestined to take place.' (Luke24:26, Acts 4:27-28)

Could Jesus have avoided the cross?
The divine appointment of the anointed Son of God is to rule the world on behalf of his Father. Yet at the very beginning of his pub-

lic ministry we read, 'Again, the devil took him to a very high mountain and showed him all the kingdoms of the world and their glory. And he said to him, "All these I will give you, if you will fall down and worship me."' All these can be yours, if you will be my servant, my deputy. That is what the invitation to 'worship' the evil one implied: all the world – without the misery, the gore, the terrible anguish of the cross. 'Then Jesus said to him, "Be gone, Satan! For it is written, 'You shall worship the Lord your God and him only shall you serve.'" (Matt 4:8-10)

When Jesus began to speak to the disciples of his arrest and being put to death, Peter rebuked him. And Peter would have defended him at his arrest, but the Lord would have none of it. Even as he was on trial before Pilate, Jesus said that he could have called on twelve legions of angels to deliver him – but he chose not to.

Jesus came to do his Father's will. He could have avoided the cross, but in total obedience to his Father, he laid aside the glory of heaven to become a man, a servant, and was obedient to death, even to death on a cross. (Philippians 2:6-8)

The unique significance of the cross of the Lord Jesus Christ lies not in the anguish, but in who it was who hung and suffered there, and in what was achieved by it.

What was accomplished by the cross of Jesus?

The cross is like a diamond with many facets from which shine out brilliant shafts of spiritual light. May I invite you to look at some of the New Testament insights? One insight will often overlap with another.

An example
The apostle Peter writing to suffering Christian believers, writes, 'Remember the One who suffered for you. When he was reviled he did not respond with curses. When he suffered he did not threaten, but committed his rightful cause to the One who ultimately judges justly.' (1 Peter 2:20-24)

The Lord's pattern of patient endurance displayed on the cross, and his willingness to plead for the Father's forgiveness of those who put him on that cross, is the pattern for those who claim to follow him. People who are no friends of New Testament Christianity, nevertheless revel in the example of Jesus. Christian believers are called to take note of it and put our Lord's pattern into practice – but not to stop there! There is more to the cross of Jesus than a pattern for godly suffering.

A sacrifice
In John the Baptist's words 'Behold the [sacrificial] Lamb of God who takes away the sin of the world.' The Cross of the Lord Jesus was a sacrifice, 'He loved us and gave himself for us a fragrant offering.' (Ephesians 5:2) This is a theme expanded in Hebrews. Hebrews draws attention to the daily priestly offering of sacrifices. They were a prophetic foreshadowing of what was to come. On the cross is the reality, the Lord Jesus, 'our holy and blameless high priest, offered up himself once and for all.' He 'put away our sin by the sacrifice of himself'. The precious death of the 'Lamb of God' for us was 'an offering and a sacrifice once and for all'. (Hebrews 7:26-27, 9:22, 10:10-14)

The New Testament speaks of God's people as being 'purchased, ransomed and redeemed'

The picture is of a debtor's prison. There is no chance of escape, nor any chance of repaying the debt we owe. But on the cross the debt has been fully paid on our behalf. In the Lord Jesus Christ, and through his cross, his believing people are redeemed and set free.

Another picture is the slave market. What chance has a branded slave got? But the Lord Jesus on that cross 'purchased' our freedom; He 'ransomed' his believing people. He '. . . ransomed people for God from every tribe and language and people and nation' by his precious blood shed on the cross of Calvary. (Revelation 5:9) Or as the apostle Peter puts it, the Lord God ransomed the people of God '. . . not with perishable things such as silver or gold, but with the precious blood of Christ, like that of a lamb without blemish or spot'. (1 Peter 1:18-19) As Jesus said of himself, 'The Son of Man came not to be served, but to serve and to give his life a ransom for many' (Mark 10:45).

On the cross the Son of God was himself a sacrificial offering to purchase, ransom and redeem his believing people.

A covering.

We use the word cover in two ways. We cover something to hide it and hope it will not be discovered. But we also use the use the word in this biblical sense when we speak of someone who has had a car accident and add, "Fortunately he was covered." We do not mean that the accident has been hidden or buried, but that someone else has agreed to bear the cost of the loss, in this case an insurance company. When the New Testament applies the word to our failures, it does not mean that they have been hidden from God's sight, but that the Lord Jesus has undertaken to bear the cost; the punishment *we* deserve. On the cross, the Lord Jesus provided a 'covering' for our failure before Almighty God; to 'cover' for our failure to honour the One in whose hand is our existence, our life and our every circumstance.

If we have really taken hold of the fact that 'the Son of God loved us and gave himself for us' – if you are one of his ransomed people – your or my utter unworthiness is 'covered.' The apostle Paul uses the word in this way as he quotes Psalm 32:1-2 'Blessed [how much to be envied] are those whose iniquities are forgiven and whose sins are covered' (Romans 4:7). No wonder the Reformers revelled in this facet of the cross. By his cross, the Lord Jesus has paid for the covering of our sin.

A cleansing place and a legal court acquittal
'And such were some of you...' writes the apostle Paul after a list of behaviours and failures before God '. . . but you were washed, you were sanctified, you were justified in the name of the Lord Jesus Christ and by the Spirit of our God.' (1 Corinthians 6:11) Another aspect of the cross found in this verse is the word 'justified'. It is a legal term. Before Almighty God we deserve to be banished, swept away; we deserve to perish. But the cross of the Lord Jesus provides God's wonderful amnesty, his free forgiveness in and through the cross of his Son. Believing in the Lord Jesus and gratefully accepting what he has done on the cross, we can stand acquitted before God. We can be declared righteous, forgiven and accepted before Almighty God, the Lord and Judge. Washed, cleansed, justified, made one of God's holy people – and 'sanctified', by the Holy Spirit of God; set on the path of holy, joyful and obedient living before God. Is that you? Is that me?

The New Testament also speaks of the cross in terms of three very large words – reconciliation, substitution and propitiation

Reconciliation

The apostle Paul writes of being 'reconciled to God' through the death of his Son. (Romans 5:8-11 and 2 Corinthians 5 18) The apostle writes of us being reconciled to God, not of him being reconciled to us, because the enmity is on our side. We are the enemies of God because of our unwillingness to live in his world in a way that honours and obeys him. However, by the cross of his Son he has provided a way of reconciliation. Speaking of the Lord Jesus he writes, 'And you, who once were alienated and hostile in mind, doing evil deeds, he has now reconciled in his body of flesh by his death . . .' (Colossians 1:21)

Substitution

How is such reconciliation brought about? By the second of these great words – by his beloved Son taking our place, and bearing the wrath and the punishment we deserve; by *substitution*. Here is a concept hated and rejected by many because it is a stab to our pride; it is humiliating. However it is a concept woven throughout the Scriptures.

In Exodus chapter 20, the Passover lamb 'took the place of' the first-born son in each Hebrew family. The lamb died, but the son was spared. The angel of death 'passed over' the households of the people of Israel where a lamb had been sacrificed. 'Christ,' writes the apostle Paul in 1 Corinthians 5 verse 7, 'our Passover [lamb] has been sacrificed'. He has taken our place.

Isaiah makes this concept even more explicit as he prophesied about the 'Suffering Servant of the Lord'. 'Surely he has borne our griefs and carried our sorrows; yet we esteemed him stricken, smitten by God, and afflicted. But he was wounded for our transgressions; he was crushed for our iniquities; upon him was the chastisement that brought us peace, with his stripes we are healed. All we like sheep have gone astray; we have turned every one to his own way; and the Lord has laid on him the iniquity of us all.' (Isaiah 53:4-6)

On the cross, the Son of God took our place. He gave himself for us. He bore the wrath and the anger of God that we deserve.

> *In my place condemned he stood;*
> *Sealed my pardon with his blood:*
> *Hallelujah! What a Saviour!*

Propitiation

John in his first letter writes, 'In this is love, not that we loved God but that he loved us and sent his Son to be the *propitiation* for our sins.' (1 John 4:10) The English word 'propitiation' means 'to change the face of.' In this setting it is to cause the Lord God to look with favour on us. His look is changed from one of justified anger towards us because of our rebellion and failure before him, to one of fatherly welcome and love, as we accept the free forgiveness he offers in the cross of his beloved Son, the Lord Jesus.

Some modern translators prefer the word 'expiation' which means a 'mopping up', a 'clearing away' of our transgressions, or the making of a satisfactory repayment for them. The underlying Greek word indicates an atoning sacrifice. The word goes back to the 'mercy seat' of the Old Testament, where on the ark, beneath the arched wings of the cherubim, was the place where God's justice and God's mercy met. As the great hymn of the Welsh revival put it;

> *Grace and love, like mighty rivers,*
> *Poured incessant from above,*
> *And heaven's peace and perfect justice*
> *Kissed a guilty world in love.*

The uniquely precious death of the Son of God on the cross of Calvary is our example of patient suffering and forgiveness of those who wrong us – and yet it is so much more. As the perfect offering and sacrifice, it secures the cleansing, washing, purchase, ransom, redemption, of all the believing sons and daughters of God. And it opens the way to a life-changing work of God in each of our lives by his Holy Spirit.

> *On the mount of crucifixion*
> *Fountains opened deep and wide;*
> *Through the floodgates of God's mercy*
> *Flowed a vast and gracious tide.*

The Lord Jesus, through his atoning death on Calvary's hill, fulfilled his own exclusive claim, 'I am the way, and the truth, and the life. No-one comes to the Father except through me.' (John 14:6)

Heavenly Father, stir us, challenge us and thrill us afresh by what you and your beloved Son have made possible in and through the cross of our Lord.

Questions for personal reflection or discussion

'The uniquely precious death of the Son of God on the cross of Calvary is our example of patient suffering and forgiveness of those who wrong us – and yet it is so much more. As the perfect offering and sacrifice, it secures the cleansing, washing, purchase, ransom, redemption, of all the believing sons and daughters of God. And it opens the way to a life-changing work of God in each of our lives by his Holy Spirit.'

1. What precious truths can we learn from each of the significant New Testament words concerning the cross?
2. Are we willing to humble ourselves and recognise our need for what lies behind each one of these New Testament descriptions of the cross?

The hymns quoted

In my place condemned he stood, a line from *Man of Sorrows!* by Philipp Bliss

Grace and love . . . ' and *On the mount of crucifixion*, lines from the hymn, *Here is love vast as the ocean* by William Rees and William Edwards

Thomas

Now Thomas, one of the twelve, called the Twin, was not with them when Jesus came. So the other disciples told him, "We have seen the Lord." But he said to them, "Unless I see in his hands the mark of the nails, and place my finger into the mark of the nails, and place my hand into his side, I will never believe."

Eight days later, his disciples were inside again, and Thomas was with them. Although the doors were locked, Jesus came and stood among them and said, "Peace be with you." Then he said to Thomas, "Put your finger here, and see my hands: and put out your hand, and place it in my side. Do not disbelieve, but believe." Thomas answered him, "My Lord and my God!" Jesus said to him, "Have you believed because you have seen me? Blessed are those who have not seen and yet have believed."

Now Jesus did many other signs in the presence of his disciples, which are not written in this book; but these are written so that you may believe that Jesus is the Christ, the Son of God, and that by believing you may have life in his name.

John 20:24-31 English Standard Version

Thomas – The Doubter Convinced

In the days following Jesus' resurrection, the disciples were very unsure of themselves. They had spent three years as disciples of Jesus. Suddenly he was arrested, falsely accused, and put to death. A few days later they were coming to terms with the reports of his resurrection. Singly and in groups, the disciples met with the risen Lord Jesus over the next forty days. Thomas missed the first occasion when the risen Lord met the disciples as a group, but was present eight days later.

Jesus had commanded the disciples to wait in Jerusalem until the promised Holy Spirit came on them and enabled them to be his witnesses in Jerusalem and to the ends of the earth.

The great missionary activity of the disciples began when they were filled and empowered by the Holy Spirit on the day of Pentecost. But here is a man reputed for his missionary activity, though not often thought about in those terms. He was famous for something else.

We know very little about Thomas. In the gospels of Matthew, Mark and Luke, Thomas is no more than a name on a list of disciples. His name comes from the Aramaic and means 'twin' and, in the gospel of John, Thomas is often referred to as 'Didymus' which is Greek for twin. Do we know anything of Thomas' twin? And the answer is – nothing at all.

Only in John's Gospel do we learn a little more, for John records some of Thomas' words. We first meet Thomas in John Chapter 11. Beginning at verse 1, 'Now a certain man was ill, Lazarus of Bethany, the village of Mary and her sister Martha . . .' (v.7), 'Jesus said to the disciples, "Let us go to Judea again." The disciples said to him, "Rabbi, the Jews were just now trying to stone you, and are you going there again?" . . .' (v.16), 'Thomas, who was called the Twin, said to his fellow-disciples, "Let us also go, that we may die with him."'

Peter was a man very forward with his words. John was a deep and thoughtful man. Thomas was a man of few words – a rather gloomy man, but a realist.

We hear of Thomas again in Chapter 14 verses 1-6. Jesus was preparing his disciples for his leaving them, and he said to them, "Do not let your hearts be troubled. Believe in God, believe also in me. In my Father's house there are many dwelling-places. If it were not so, would I have told you that I go to prepare a place for you? And if I go and prepare a place for you, I will come again and will take you to myself, so that where I am, there you may be also. And you know the way to the place where I am going." Thomas said to him, "Lord, we do not know where you are going. How can we know the way?" Jesus said to him, "I am the way, and the truth, and the life. No one comes to the Father except through me."

Thomas was a consistent man, a realist and a brave man, willing to say what many would have passed over with a nod of the head. Thomas said in effect, 'We have not got any idea where you are going, how can we follow you?' In a very few words, Thomas was willing to say what others would not feel able to say. I'm grateful to Thomas for the example of his outspoken honesty, and his willingness to appear to his fellow disciples, and to his teacher, to be rather slow and unintelligent. However, I am even more grateful to Thomas for the famous and precious answer that Thomas' words drew from Jesus: "I am the way, and the truth, and the life. No one comes to the Father except through me." (verse 6)

How reassuring those words are to those who believe. If you have a vital, God-given and obedient faith built on the person, the commandments and the promises of the Son of God, the Lord Jesus, you have built on a sure foundation. But how terrifying those words are to those who are hoping to enter the kingdom of heaven by another way, by-passing the Lord Jesus, his cross, and a life of obedience to him.

These are very significant and precious words, provoked by Thomas. It is one of a number of very significant sayings in the gospel of John.

Does Thomas do it again? Yes, he does. We next read of him in Chapter 20 verses 19-29 'When it was evening on that day, the first day of the week, and the doors of the house where the disciples had met were locked for fear of the Jews, Jesus came and stood among them . . .' v.24 But Thomas (who was called the Twin), one of the twelve, was not with them when Jesus came. So the other disciples told him, "We have seen the Lord." But he said to them, "Unless I see the mark of the nails in his hands, and put my finger in the mark of the nails and my hand in his side, I will not believe."

It was the Sunday evening, the day of the resurrection when Jesus showed himself to the disciples. But, for some unknown reason, Thomas was not there. Having clearly seen the possibility of Jesus' arrest and death, and then seen it take place, perhaps he did not want company. Perhaps he wanted to be alone. Anyway, Thomas was not there. When the disciples told Thomas that Jesus was risen, Thomas seemed almost angry with himself for not being there and made this extremely strong statement, "Unless I see the mark of the nails in his hands, and put my finger in the mark of the nails and my hand in his side, I will not believe."

In the circumstances, perhaps we can understand Thomas and that over-strong statement of disbelief. But I'm so grateful to Thomas. He was not gullible. He was not one to be swept along by the enthusiasm and euphoria of his fellow disciples. Thomas was a realist, and he demanded clear evidence.

Then, verses 26-29: 'A week later his disciples were again in the house, and Thomas was with them. Although the doors were shut, Jesus came and stood among them and said, "Peace be with you." Then he said to Thomas, "Put your finger here, and see my hands: and put out your hand, and place it in my side. Do not disbelieve, but believe." Thomas answered him, "My Lord and my God!" Jesus said to him, "Have you believed because you have seen me? Blessed are those who have not seen and yet have believed."

The Lord knows our secret and our declared thoughts. How wonderfully our Lord meets us where we are, with all our questions and doubts. These are the final few recorded words of Thomas, "My Lord and my God!" They are very significant words, they clearly indicate that Thomas, the doubter, was totally convinced. It is the high point of the Gospel of John. Thomas the doubter's words of confession declare who Jesus really is, God among us, Emmanuel, and they set the seal on the resurrection of the Son of God.

Lastly, look at Jesus' final beatitude. The beatitudes are recorded by both Matthew and Luke, Here is a sample of them from Matthew, 'Blessed are the poor in spirit, for theirs is the kingdom of heaven.' 'Blessed are those who mourn, for they shall be comforted.' 'Blessed are the meek, for they shall inherit the earth . . .' And, here in the gospel of John, is our Lord's final beatitude. Again, the words were drawn from Jesus by 'Doubting Thomas.' Jesus said to him, "Have you believed because you have seen me? Blessed are those who have not seen and yet have believed."

This is a word for us to take to heart in our doubting generation. It is our Lord's final beatitude "Blessed, are those who have not seen and yet have believed". We will never take hold of the wonder and strength of the word 'blessed' until we understand that as well as meaning 'happy', it means, 'how 'much to be envied' are those who have not seen and yet believe.'

Thomas now disappears from the New Testament writings and from our view. But not quite, for this same Thomas has a reputation in ancient history and legend. It seems that Thomas' confession was no passing belief, put down to a moment of high emotion and soon forgotten. Thomas' faith was deep, life-long and it bore fruit.

It is claimed that it was Thomas who first took the gospel to Elam, Persia or as it is now, Iran, and it was Thomas who first preached the gospel and founded churches in India.

For us, India sounds a long way for a first century disciple to travel. But in Thomas' day there were trading ships that plied the Red Sea to and from India – they brought back rare spices, such as, the valuable flask of pure nard that Mary poured over Jesus at Bethany.

The Malabar and Ma Thoma Christians in South West India look back with gratitude to the disciple Thomas and hold fast to their understanding that it was Thomas who, travelling on a trading ship, brought the gospel to them.

Thomas, a man of very few words. Thomas, a man who brought wonderful and challenging words from our Lord's lips. Thomas, the doubter convinced, who we are told went on to live for his Lord and God as a missionary.

Heavenly Father, give us grace to learn from Thomas, Thomas the realist, Thomas the doubter convinced, Thomas the active believer bringing the Gospel to others.

Questions for personal reflection or discussion

1. It is usual to think of Thomas as the great doubter, but do we have cause to be grateful to him?
2. As Jesus was determined to return to Jerusalem, it was obvious to the disciples what might happen, but only Thomas was willing to say it. Should we be grateful to those who are bold and brave enough to put into words the doubts, and the fears, and the forebodings that many of us secretly feel, but would not dare to say publicly?
3. None of the disciples really understood where Jesus was going or how they could follow him. Can it be hard to admit such ignorance? Does it take courage to put it into words, especially in front of other people?
4. We do not know why Thomas was absent when our risen Lord first met with the disciples. But can you understand something of why he might have given such an over strong statement of unwillingness to believe?
5. Thomas certainly cannot be accused of being swept along by the enthusiasm of the other disciples. After such determined unwillingness to believe, can Thomas's confession of Jesus as 'My Lord and my God!' be a help and encouragement to us when tempted to question or doubt?
6. As a doubter convinced, can Thomas's reputation for taking the gospel to others be an encouragement and challenge to us?

Pentecost Then and Now

When the day of Pentecost arrived, they [the disciples] were all together in one place. And suddenly there came from heaven a sound like a mighty rushing wind, and it filled the entire house where they were sitting. And divided tongues as of fire appeared to them and rested on each one of them. And they were all filled with the Holy Spirit and began to speak in other tongues as the Spirit gave them utterance. And at this sound the multitude came together and they were bewildered, because each one was hearing them speak in his own language, "We hear them telling in our own tongues the mighty works of God, What does this mean?"

But Peter standing with the eleven, lifted up his voice . . . "Let all the house of Israel therefore know for certain that God has made him both Lord and Christ, this Jesus whom you crucified."

Now when they heard this they were cut to the heart, and said to Peter and to the rest of the apostles, "Brothers, what shall we do?" And Peter said to them, "Repent and be baptized every one of you in the name of Jesus Christ for the forgiveness of your sins, and you will receive the gift of the Holy Spirit. For the promise is for you and your children and for all who are far off, everyone whom the Lord our God calls to himself." And he continued to exhort them. So those who received his word were baptized, and there were added that day about three thousand souls. And they devoted themselves to the apostles' teaching and fellowship, to the breaking of bread and the prayers.

Verses from Acts 2:1-42 English Standard Version

Pentecost Then and Now

I have something quite surprising to say. For, as with a preacher, so with a writer on the things of God, I have to confess that of myself I have nothing useful to offer you!

I have words in my mind which might interest, inform and fill the pages, but they are worth nothing. Unless, that is, Almighty God chooses to take and speak through them by his Holy Spirit. Only then will there be an awareness of the felt presence of God which will stir our hearts, our minds and our wills, so that we turn, repent, believe and pledge ourselves afresh to the ways and service of the living God.

That is exactly what happened on the day of Pentecost, as Peter, filled with the Holy Spirit of God, addressed the gathered crowd.

A work of God, not of ourselves

Jesus had said to the disciples, "If you love me, you will keep my commandments. And I will ask the Father, and he will give you another Helper (The Greek can also be translated 'Advocate' or 'Counsellor'), to be with you for ever, even the Spirit of truth, whom the world cannot receive, because it neither sees him nor knows him. You know him, for he dwells with you and will be in you." (John 14:16-17). This is what makes the true people of God distinct. It is the hallmark of God's people – God at work in our lives and through our lives by his Holy Spirit.

Jesus' promise was fulfilled at Pentecost. Puzzled and uncertain disciples, wondering whether to go back to fishing, were waiting in Jerusalem as Jesus had commanded them. They had gathered to pray and encourage one another, and together to seek the Lord's will. Suddenly they were filled with the Holy Spirit and made bold men of God, telling out the 'mighty works of God' in languages they had never learnt. That, together with the sound as of a mighty wind, was the spectacular act of God that drew the city and its feast-time visitors to hear Peter.

Peter simply proclaimed who Jesus truly is, and what had happened to him by the hand of their leaders.

The Lord God by his Holy Spirit continued the sovereign work he had begun with 'the sound as of a mighty wind' and 'tongues as of fire'. The Lord God took Peter's words – and his hearers heard, not so much Peter's words, but a word of judgement from the Lord, and a clear declaration of the way of forgiveness.

The Lord God took Peter's words and applied them to the minds and hearts and wills of those who heard him speak, and they were 'cut to the heart'; convicted of the truth of the charge that Peter laid at their feet.

Under the power of God, and acknowledging the truth of Peter's words, they cried out, "What shall we do?" And Peter urged them repent and believe on the crucified Son of God, the Messiah, and be baptised in his name. And hearing this, those who had been 'cut to the heart' turned in repentance and faith, were baptised and received the gift of the Holy Spirit at work in and through their lives. At Pentecost, God's true church was born.

Pentecost, a challenge for ourselves in our own day

We too need to see the Lord God at work in and through faithful preaching and church leadership, and in and through the lives of believing people.

In the Old Testament, Moses is recorded pleading with God to continue to be with his people, and to go before them: "If your presence will not go with me, do not bring us up from here. For how shall it be known that I have found favour in your sight, I and your people? Is it not in your going with us, so that we are distinct, I and your people, from every other people on the face of the earth?" (Exodus 33:15-16)

What is it that makes the true people of God distinct? It is not that they are 'decent people', 'respectable people' or 'church-going people'. Nor is it a sense of destiny, let alone a feeling of superiority. It is the Lord God himself, known and seen and felt to be among his people by the Holy Spirit. It is the awesome awareness of the presence of God; the hand of God on both preacher and hearers alike. As it was with the early church, we will be aware of it ourselves, and so will those around us. The Lord God and his Son, by the Holy Spirit, use our simple words and simple deeds of kindness to enlighten minds, and to touch and change lives in, and among, and through his people. This is the essence of Pentecost, both then and now.

What a challenge to the modern church. Do we, do you know anything of these things? Have we, have you, known a work of God in our lives causing us to turn, repent, believe and be forgiven? Have we, have I, have you been brought to life by the Holy Spirit, and made a member of God's people?

That is what happened to a great number of Peter's hearers on the Day of Pentecost. And it did not stop there, as if it was some passing experience. Luke records, 'They devoted themselves to the apostles' teaching and fellowship, to the breaking of bread and the prayers.'

It is a mark of God's Holy Spirit enlightening our minds, stirring our hearts, and making us willing to change our ways, that we begin to be hungry for the Apostles' teaching – physically listened to by the people in the days after Pentecost and now written for us in the New Testament. It is a mark of the Holy Spirit at work, when we begin to love to meet with fellow believers to pray, and to encourage one another to apply the teachings of the apostles, written for us in the New Testament, to our lives in the world of today.

Pentecost, the Birthday of the Church. Have we tasted any of these things? Do we long and earnestly pray that our local church might be (as God's intention for it is), not just a nice place to meet our friends and hear an interesting talk – but a foretaste of the kingdom of heaven?

The people of God are born of his Holy Spirit to be living the kingdom life, telling out 'the mighty works of God' – here and now, in our own city, town or village. If this were truly so, there would be no risk of our churches and chapels closing, as there is for so many. Each church, each chapel would become a magnet, like the early church; 'God adding to their number, daily, weekly, monthly, those who are being saved.'

Pentecost, a challenge for preachers and church leaders
Many churches in our own day seem, from a human and organisational point of view, to manage very well with very little reference to God, let alone in utter dependence on him. It is almost as if the minister and people are completely unaware of the essential ingredient so close to Moses' heart; 'the presence of God in and among his people', and especially the hand of God on the leaders.

There are many very competent speakers in our churches and chapels, but speakers who 'speak as from the Lord' as the apostle Peter did, are very rare.

It is not a matter of 'force of personality', loudness, theatrical skills or skill in public speaking. Anointed preaching, like that of

Peter on the Day of Pentecost, may be very quietly and humbly spoken, even falteringly spoken, but those who hear are aware that the words have the supernatural seal of the Lord God's ownership on them.

In days of revival it was common to read of ministers secretly in their room before going up the pulpit steps to preach, spending time on their knees earnestly pleading with the Lord to go before them and be with them and take their words and use them for his glory. Praying very much like Moses did, "If your presence will not go with me, do not bring us up from here."

May I conclude with the words of Robert Key, a man greatly used of God in the 1800s.

'I am deeply convinced that the want of the times is, a ministry clothed with power from on high, whatever other attainments may be possessed. There may be learning, talent, eloquence – and we do not undervalue these – but nothing can ever qualify a man for extensive usefulness in the church and in the world except the Divine "anointing," the "unction from the Holy One," . . .'

Heavenly Father, thank you for Pentecost, the Birthday of your Church, and we pray that the centuries may not dim our vision. And that you, by your Holy Spirit, would fulfil your purposes, revive your church, stir your people, and make each gathering of Christians a beacon, like a city set on a hill – for the glory of your name. Amen.

Questions for personal reflection or discussion

1. In most places of worship you will find delightful, helpful and charming people, but what should be the distinguishing feature of the true people of God?

2. There will always be many good folk attracted to a church or chapel, but in our own church is there a core of people who love and serve the Lord and are truly on fire for him and the kingdom of heaven?

3. Could we honestly say that we are aware of the Lord God's presence among us as a fellowship? Could we say that of ourselves personally?

4. Typically when thinking of Pentecost we concentrate on the spectacular; the sound of a mighty rushing wind, tongues as of fire and the disciples telling out the mighty works of God in languages that they had never learnt. But that is not the whole picture. The whole picture would include the God-anointed preaching of Peter, and the humbling hand of God on the hearers so that they were 'cut to the heart'. Should we consider the whole day to be the beginning of a mighty work of God, and long and pray that such a work of God might be repeated in our own day?

5. Robert Key would urge us to join him in praying that the Lord God would raise up Holy Spirit-anointed preachers like Peter in our own day. Should we? Do we earnestly seek God's face in this respect?

The Trinity

There's a knock on the door or a ring at the bell and a couple of courteous people standing on your doorstep asking for your opinion on the way things are going – the state of the world, the wars and climate change. "Are you prepared for the end of the world? May we give you a leaflet and invite you to a meeting?"

They are to be commended for their boldness and a very good opening question. But you guess that, although they may encourage you to join them, they cannot help you find a truly biblical faith. You tell them you attend a local church, and in conversation, the Trinity is mentioned, and they assure you that the Trinity is not found in the Bible. It is a false church teaching.

But that is a half truth masking the fact that they are being 'economical' with the whole truth. It is perfectly true that the word 'Trinity' is not found in the Bible. You can search for it from end to end and you will not find it. However, and it is a rather significant 'however'. If you really read Scripture you will find – not that we have made up a theory – but that the Lord God has chosen to reveal himself as one and yet three, three and yet one. Three distinct and separate persons, and yet one God:

– God the Father, who, together with his Son brought the universe, including this beautiful planet, into existence.

– God the Son, Emmanuel, who humbled himself, laid aside the glory of heaven and became one of us. He chose to fulfil his Father's will, and was obedient even to death on the cross. Why? For our rescue. The Son of God has borne the punishment we deserve for failing to honour and obey the One in whose hand is our very existence and our every circumstance – our health, our wealth, our breath. As God's prophet Isaiah put it, 'All we like sheep have gone astray; we have turned every one to our own way; and the Lord has laid on him the iniquity of us all.' Or in the words of the apostle Paul, 'The Son of God loved me and gave himself for me.'

– God the Father, by whose will this universe was brought into existence. God the Son, who laid aside the glory of heaven and became a man, giving his life for our rescue. And God the Holy Spirit, who brings to life the people of God. He it is who opens spiritually blind eyes to see the wonder of the kingdom of God. He unstops spiritually deaf ears to hear the word of the Lord, and turns the printed page of Scripture into the living word of God. Those whose eyes are opened and ears unstopped love it, read it, feed on it and are nourished by it.

God the Father, God the Son and God the Holy Spirit – the Trinity, One God yet three persons.

There are things in the natural world that to a limited extent help us to grasp the concept of the Trinity: We typically find three distinct lobes on a single leaf of clover. Or one substance, for example water, in three distinct forms: as a vapour (mist, steam or moisture in the air); as a liquid (water); as a solid (ice). Or, the charcoal used as fuel for your barbecue, the graphite, referred to as 'lead' in your pencil, and the diamond in your ring, again, these are three separate and distinct forms of one substance – carbon.

Reading the Bible as a whole, the Trinity becomes, not an abstract theory, but the vital reality of the one God you know, who has made himself known as three distinct persons. Taught by Scripture, enlightened by the Holy Spirit, you will find evidence of the Trinity on page after page. These are not 'proof texts' so much as 'foot prints' or 'fingerprints'.

Open the Bible at Genesis 1:1. 'In the beginning God . . .' To the distress of those who do not accept the divinity of the Lord Jesus, word for 'God' in the original Hebrew, and the references to him, are plural, as they is all through this chapter; for example verse 26, 'Let us make man in our image.' – Open it at the gospel of John 1:1. 'In the beginning was the Word, and the Word was with God, and the Word was God. He was in the beginning with God. All things were made through him, and without him was not anything made that was made . . . and the Word became flesh and dwelt among us full of grace and truth.' As the apostle makes clear, 'The Word' is the Lord Jesus. – Open the Bible at Colossians 2:9, '. . . in whom dwells all the fullness of the Godhead bodily.' God in a human body. The apostle Paul is referring to the Lord Jesus. – Open it at St John chapter 20:28, 'My Lord and my God,' confessed the finally, fully convinced doubting Thomas as he came face to face with his risen Lord.

The Holy Spirit has similar marks of his divine nature throughout Scripture. In the New Testament he is referred to as the Spirit, the Holy Spirit, the Spirit of God, the Spirit of Jesus, quite interchangeably.

And there are so many more 'fingerprints', including these two very familiar ones, (2 Corinthians 13:14) 'The grace of our Lord Jesus Christ and the love of God and the fellowship of the Holy Spirit . . .' And our Lord's great commission to 'Go and make disciples of all nations, baptizing them in the name' – the word 'name' is singular – 'in the name of the Father and of the Son and of the

Holy Spirit, teaching them to observe all that I have commanded you . . .' (Matthew 28:18-20)

This is only a glimpse of the Scriptural foundation that underlies the Christian understanding of God as three distinct persons and yet one God, and a few illustrations from the natural world. But scholars could furnish you with many books or lectures on the vigorous debates that have taken place through the centuries concerning the Trinity. They will tell you of the Arians, who did not accept the divinity of Christ, and of Athanasius who stood against the world of his day to defend this scriptural teaching that we know as the Trinity. They will tell you of the many heresies that have sprung up around the Trinity and of the great councils of Nicaea and Constantinople, where the church fathers hammered out an understanding of the Trinity that was both according to Scripture and could be widely accepted among Christian people.

The Trinity – to know the truth behind this simple word is heavenly treasure:

– To know God the Father as our holy, righteous and loving heavenly Father.

– To know God the Son as our Prophet, Priest and King, Saviour and Lord, Friend, Shepherd and Guide.

– To know something of the presence and work of God the Holy Spirit in our lives, and in the lives of those around us.

This has been the privilege of the saints of God through the running centuries.

Father, the Trinity is always a mystery. Some will treat it with contempt, some will question it. By your grace, may we rejoice in the underlying truth of it.

Questions for personal reflection or discussion

1. The Trinity is not an understanding of the nature of the Lord God that we find to be naturally easy to grasp or accept. Is it something we struggle with ourselves?

2. Have you met people who flatly deny it and would have you join a group of like-minded people?

3. Reading the Bible as a whole, the Trinity becomes, not an abstract theory, but the vital reality of the one God you know, who has made himself known as three distinct persons. Taught by Scripture, enlightened by the Holy Spirit, you will find evidence of the Trinity on page after page. They are not 'proof texts' so much as 'foot prints' or 'fingerprints'. Has that proved true for yourself?

4. The felt presence of God among us. The Lord Jesus with us, prompting and leading us. The Holy Spirit doing his sovereign work among the people of God. Have you known any of these things personally in your life or in the life of a local church?

Paul in Athens

Now while Paul was waiting for them in Athens, his spirit was provoked within him as he saw that the city was full of idols. So he reasoned in the synagogue with the Jews and the devout persons, and in the market place every day with those who happened to be there. Some of the Epicurean and Stoic philosophers also conversed with him. And some said, "What does this babbler wish to say?" Others said, "He seems to be a preacher of foreign divinities" – because he was preaching Jesus and the resurrection. And they took hold of him and brought him to the Areopagus, saying, "May we know what this new teaching is that you are presenting? For you bring some strange things to our ears. We wish to know therefore what these things mean."

Acts 17:16-20 English Standard Version

Paul's time in Athens

Why was the apostle in Athens?
To answer that, we need to step back a little in time. Paul was now on his second missionary journey. After disagreeing with Paul, Barnabas had left for Cyprus taking with him Mark. A little later, with the prayers and blessing of the church at Antioch, Paul and Silas were sent out to preach and to encourage the believers Paul had met on his first journey with Barnabas.

The apostle was very sensitive to the leading of the Holy Spirit, and so, although he intended to visit an area of north western Turkey then known as 'Asia', he found himself spiritually barred. However, under the hand of God, he had a vision of a man in mainland Europe, begging him to come over and help. So together with Silas and joined by Luke (this is the first of the 'we' passages recorded in Acts) they came to Philippi, where the Lord stirred Lydia's heart to heed the gospel and become one of the first European believers. Very dramatically, the Lord God also brought the Philippian jailer and his household to faith. (Acts6:6-24)

Obliged to leave Philippi, Paul and Silas went on their way first to Thessalonica and then to Berea. From both of these cities Paul was forced out by the violence of those who opposed his message. The believers in Berea took care of Paul and, for his safety, escorted him by ship some 300 miles down the coast to Athens, where Paul waited for Silas and Timothy to join him.

What was Athens like?
Athens was the great university city of the ancient world and the centre of Greek culture and philosophical thought. It was a magnet which drew senior academics and intellectuals from across the ancient world. They would gather in Athens to entertain one another with the latest news, theory or philosophical gossip. They did not tend to be seekers after truth, but were ready to hear and give their opinion on any subject that came to their attention. (Beware, for the Holy Spirit rarely makes God's gospel truth impact us if, like these men, we have a purely academic interest in his word.)

The city of Athens was filled with shrines to Greek gods and goddesses, but displayed a desperately sad ignorance of the one true God. Paul found himself stirred by the Holy Spirit and by what he saw, and set about proclaiming, debating, and persuading all who would hear him, of the truths of God and of his risen Son, the Lord Jesus Christ. He did so in the synagogue, and every day in the market place.

Some of the Athenian philosophers heard him. The Epicurians held that this life was essentially all there is, and that it should be filled with that which gives the greatest contentment. The Stoics, in contrast. taught a kind of pantheism, teaching that life should be lived in accord with 'the all-pervading divine,' and lived in a way that was quite detached, quite unmoved, by either pain or pleasure.' (Hence, what we call Stoicism.) Paul's gospel message cut across both the practical atheism of the Epicurians and the pantheism of the Stoics, as he called for submission and obedience to the one true God and his risen and soon returning Son; the Lord and Judge of all.

How did the philosophers react?
"What is this babbler saying?" Notice the implied, self-confident superiority. (Like the seed sown on the pathway in Jesus' parable of the sower, such an attitude of heart all but guarantees a stony reception to the word of God.) They didn't actually say 'babbler'. In the Greek they refer to him as 'this ignorant plagiarist', 'this peasant with not an original thought in his head'. And further, Paul's subject, 'Jesus and the resurrection', led to a misunderstanding. He was accused of announcing new, or strange, gods, the Greek puts it more strongly, 'foreign demons'. In the Greek, 'the resurrection' is

'anastasin,' and you may have met ladies called Anastasia, so to the Athenians it sounded as if Paul was proclaiming Jesus and some new Greek goddess.

'They took Paul.' Did they arrest him, or just escort him? We don't know. The Greek simply says, 'taking hold of him they led him to the Areopagus'. Athens is dramatically hilly. The Acropolis is a great hill, and the Areopagus is a spur of land from the same land mass, and is called the hill of Ares, which is Greek for the hill of Mars, or as the King James version puts it, Mars hill. On the hill of Ares stood the place of cultured debate: the Athenian parliament, the supreme court, the debating place of top intellectual people. It is not clear whether Paul was brought before a court, or whether he was brought there because it was away from the bustle of the market place and the best place for the leading men of the city to hear him explain the 'strange things coming to their ears'.

What was the apostle's approach?
Some time ago, a friend challenged me to 'think what you need to say, think to whom you are saying it, and, think how best to put it to them.' That is very wise advice. The Athenian elite had already accused Paul of being ignorant. But actually being a well-educated man who was seeking to win arrogant, sophisticated, godless pagans for the Lord, Paul did not start from Old Testament prophesies, as he might have done if seeking to win Jewish people, but from the world in which these pagan Athenians were living. He did so from the insights of their own poets and from their own understanding that they were in some way 'the offspring of God', creative and god-like.

Luke gives us a very compressed summary of Paul's sermon. As he addressed the members of the Areopagus, the apostle led them to see that they were answerable to a God they had yet to come to know. He did so by way of the dedication of one of their own shrines, 'To an Unknown God.' Paul went on to point them away from the many imaginary gods of Greek culture and to speak of the One True God, the Maker and Lord of heaven and earth. He is the One who – whether we like to acknowledge it or not – has in his hand our life, our breath, and all our circumstances. Paul explained that this One True God, then as now, commands everyone everywhere to turn, to submit to him. On the Lord God's chosen day, he will judge all the inhabitants of the earth in righteousness. He has appointed his Son, the man Christ Jesus, as Lord and Judge. On behalf of his Father, he will call everyone to account for the one life entrusted to them. (Acts 17:22-31)

For the people of Athens, that day was as yet future, as it is for us, but it is no less certain. The day of judgement will take place. The Lord God has given proof of the truth of this call to repent, to submit, believe and to obey, by the resurrection of his Son, the Lord Jesus from the dead.

How did these leading citizens of Athens respond?
On hearing Paul speak of the resurrection, predictably, some of those hearing him openly scoffed, some shielded themselves from any need to respond by saying, "We'll hear you again on this." But just a precious few, God's chosen ones, believed, among them Dionysius and Damaris are named. We know nothing about Damaris. Dionysius was an Areopagite, a member of this elite upper council of Athens. (Acts 17:32-34)

If, before God, we are willing to share the gospel with others, we may find a similar range of responses. Don't be surprised, and don't be discouraged!

Some Christian commentators have suggested that Paul's time in Athens was, 'a poor showing'. 'Paul was being too intellectual, too clever'. But I wonder if that is fair. Paul was addressing the intellectual and political leaders of Athens, and as Paul himself wrote, 'not many wise . . . powerful . . . or noble' people come to believe. They tend to be proud and self-confident, and so it is very hard and very humbling for such people to admit that they need to submit and learn something new.

Dionysius was an Areopagite, a leading man in Athens, a man of position and influence, a Supreme Court judge. What a marvellous work of God and trophy of grace to win such a man by the mere foolishness of faithful Christian preaching. There are not many preachers given the privilege of winning for the Lord, a High Court Judge, a Vice-Chancellor of a university or a member of the House of Lords.

I believe it was God's elect Lady, Selina, Countess of Huntingdon, who was a member of the House of Lords, a peer, and a very active and influential 18th century Christian believer, who used to praise God for the letter 'm' in many, so that Paul's words to the Corinthians read 'not many' – rather than 'not any' – wise, powerful or noble people are called of God. (1 Cor. 1:26) The Countess of Huntingdon was one, Dionysius was another.

Although it is said that Dionysius went on to become a great church leader, a bishop in Athens, in the writings of the apostle Paul we don't read of a church in Athens. Whatever the truth may be, under the hand of God, I don't think Paul's time in Athens was wasted. Do you?

For ourselves? What will our response be? Will we, like many of the Athenian elite, stand aloof? Will we openly – or privately and inwardly – scoff? Or will we be 'happy to hear more' – and, perhaps yet again, defer any willingness to humble ourselves and submit to the Lord God and his risen, reigning and soon returning Son, our Lord Jesus? Or will we, like Damaris and Dionysius, Lydia and the Philippian jailer, believe and be hungry to learn more?

Heavenly Father we thank you for this record of the apostle Paul's time in Athens. Grant by your Holy Spirit that we may understand and take hold of the gospel's great challenge to be right with you, humbly walking with you, trusting you, obeying you, and looking forward to that great and yet terrifying day when your Son will return as Lord and Judge of each one of us.

Questions for personal reflection or discussion

1. Obliged to leave Philippi, Paul and Silas went on their way first to Thessalonica and then to Berea. From both of these cities Paul was forced out by the violence of those who opposed his message. Has this opposition to the Christian message always been the way through the running centuries? Have we seen or tasted anything of it ourselves?

2. The apostle was very sensitive to the leading of the Holy Spirit, and so, although he intended to visit an area of north western Turkey then known as 'Asia', he found himself spiritually barred. However, under the hand of God, he had a vision of a man in mainland Europe, begging him to come over and help. Have we known anything of the 'hand of God' on our lives, leading and guiding us?

3. Paul found himself stirred by the Holy Spirit and by what he saw, and set about proclaiming, debating, and persuading all who would hear him, of the truths of God and of his risen Son, the Lord Jesus Christ. He did so in the synagogue and every day in the market place. Do we find ourselves stirred by what we see around us in our society, or in our churches? What can and should we do about it?

4. Some Christian commentators have suggested that Paul's time in Athens was 'a poor showing'. 'Paul was being too intellectual, too clever'. But I wonder if that is fair. What do you think?

5. For ourselves? What will our response be? Will we, like many of the Athenian elite, stand aloof? Will we openly – or privately and inwardly – scoff? Or will we be 'happy to hear more' – and, perhaps yet again, defer any willingness to humble ourselves and submit to the Lord God and his risen, reigning and soon returning Son, our Lord Jesus? Or will we, like Damaris and Dionysius, Lydia and the Philippian jailer, believe and long to know more?

Paul in Corinth

For consider your calling, brothers; not many of you were wise according to worldly standards, not many were powerful, not many were of noble birth. But God chose what is foolish in the world to shame the wise; God chose what is weak in the world to shame the strong; God chose what is low and despised in the world, things that are not, to bring to nothing things that are, so that no one might boast in the presence of God.
1 Corinthians 1:26-29 English Standard Version

God's ways and our ways

Not many were powerful, not many were of noble birth
It is said that the Puritan Richard Sibbes, as he lay dying, was summoned by the king's messenger to attend court for trial. He had to reply that he could not come, and added, that he was going to a place where few kings and rich men come. In our country, king Edward 6th was one, Queen Victoria another, and our late Queen Elizabeth 2nd another. As already mentioned, the rich, noble and influential Selina, Countess of Huntingdon, was humbly grateful to be counted among the members of the household of God.

By the grace of God there are some who are powerful, rich and noble, but they are few. God's ways are not ours.

Human wisdom demands that when we set out to found a new venture or movement, we gather the rich, the famous and the most influential people we can. But the Lord God's ways are very different. The Lord Jesus, in order to conquer the world with the gospel of the kingdom of God, chose twelve disciples including: 'ignorant and unlearned' fishermen, as they were described by the religious leaders in Jerusalem; a tax gatherer for the Roman conquerors, Matthew; a political activist, Simon the zealot; and one, Judas, who went on to betray him.

'For my thoughts are not your thoughts, neither are your ways my ways, declares the Lord. For as the heavens are higher than the earth, so are my ways higher than your ways and my thoughts than your thoughts.' Isaiah 55:8-9

When, as a family, we moved from Greater Manchester to rural Norfolk, we found ourselves among some very powerful and influential people. There was an MP, very soon to be awarded a life peerage, two Members of the European Parliament, a Commander, a Colonel, and a titled Lady.

Next door to us was another very influential person. She lived in a tiny cottage with two small bedrooms upstairs, and a living room and kitchen downstairs. There was no running water, simply a pump outside and a small, separate building housing what was known as a 'thunder box'; a bench with a hole. She lived there with her son, her son's wife and her two almost grown-up grandsons. She had had a very hard life. Some sixty years earlier she had become a single mother, and in those days shame was heaped on such people and very spiteful things said about both her and her son.

These were her circumstances, and here is the paradox. Laura had hardly a penny and yet, despised as she was, she was very rich.

She was one of God's chosen ones, and despite her past, had been washed, sanctified, justified and made a child of God. She was one of the most saintly people I have ever known. She read and knew her Bible and walked very closely with her Lord.

Her riches were hidden from the world, but secure in heaven. All but house-bound as she soon became, quietly and from her room, Laura was the powerhouse of the local chapel and the local church. Not by her preaching, or by financial support, but by her prayers and by her person. People would visit her and find themselves, not drained, but spiritually refreshed and encouraged. Laura took every opportunity to build up, strengthen and encourage the people of God.

The power of weakness – God's ways are not our ways.

The apostle Paul in Corinth
And when I came to you . . . I did not come proclaiming to you the testimony of God to you with lofty speech or wisdom. For I decided to know nothing among you except Jesus Christ, and him crucified. And I was with you in weakness and in fear and in much trembling, and my speech and my message were not in plausible words of wisdom, but in demonstration of the Spirit and of power, that your faith might rest not in the wisdom of men but in the power of God.
                    1 Corinthians chapter 2:1-5 English Standard Version

Paul had been brought to Athens to escape from the ire and fury of the Jewish leaders who were determined to kill him. He was brought by ship some 300 miles south to Athens, the centre of Greek philosophy and sophistication. Paul's spirit was stirred when he saw that despite the sophistication of the Athenians, the city was filled with shrines and idols. So he preached the gospel in the synagogues and daily in the market place. In Athens, Paul was given a rough ride, a tough time. (Acts 17:16-17)

From there he travelled to Corinth, the centre of Greek commerce and power, the city from which the Romans ruled. It was a city where every vice and perversion was welcomed, practised and catered for.

The apostle had been sent out with the prayers of the saints at Antioch, with the charge of preaching to the Gentile world the apparent foolishness of the cross of a crucified, and to them foreign, Saviour, a Jewish person.

So Paul came to Corinth as a fleeing refugee stripped of status or standing. Just a migrant preacher with what must have been to their ears a strange and feeble sounding message.

At that level, no wonder Paul came to Corinth in fear and trembling.

Yet at a deeper level, the apostle knew that the message of a crucified Saviour, weak as it sounded, was the power of God for the salvation, for the rescue, of all those who believe, both Jew and Gentile.

So Paul came to came to Corinth in much human weakness with fear and trembling, and yet he came commissioned of God and charged with the proclamation of the cross of Christ. Paul determined to know nothing among the citizens of Corinth except the Lord Jesus Christ and him crucified. Why? Because in that God-given message lies the power of God.

The Lord God has so ordered things that his power to touch and transform the lives of men and women, to rescue them, to make them nothing less than new creations in his Son, lies not in eloquent, lofty words of human wisdom. It lies in this simple message and call to turn from self-centred, self pleasing ways to God-centred, obedient, godly ways, and to believe on his crucified, risen and soon returning Son the Lord Jesus and so be put right with God, in Henry Lyte's words, 'ransomed, healed restored forgiven.'

Friends, I have to tell you that this is God's challenge to the most respectable of us just as much as to those who have fallen far. We each need to ask ourselves, "Where do I stand?" Without repentance toward the Lord God and faith in his Son, there is no vital walk with our heavenly Father and his Son, the Lord Jesus, no secure hope of forgiveness, no sure hope of heaven.

That is the message the apostle was charged to proclaim in Corinth, and it is the message every true herald of God is called to proclaim today.

The apostle Paul himself was a very able and extremely well educated man. However, the apostle used every portion, scrap and part of his great learning, not for a display of his eloquence, erudition and ability, not as our Bible puts it, with a display of lofty words of wisdom. The whole of Paul, his person, his speech, his ability and his learning, was put in second place. Paul's calling and his greatest desire was to be used of God, and for the glory of God alone.

In the Corinthian church there were a number of self-confident, self-appointed 'super apostles' who, by attracting followers to themselves and their own teaching, were undermining the ministry of Paul. This was an issue Paul had to address as he wrote to the Christians at Corinth. The Lord God's power is most gloriously seen, not through our ability, skill and self-confidence, but through our weakness. The kind of weakness that drives us to our knees before God and throws us in total dependence upon his wisdom, enabling and strength. 'Without me,' said our Lord Jesus, 'you can do nothing.' Nothing that is, of eternal value.

In times past, when the Lord God was pleased to send revival, it was not uncommon to read of men who, before preaching, would be found on their knees pleading with God to go before them and with them; to take their feeble words and use them for his glory.

That's a word for preachers, but what of ourselves?
God's true church is not to be like a cruise liner with a captain, crew and many passengers, but more like a sailing dingy where every person has a part to play.

After a Christian gathering, with the words of hymns, prayers, and a passage of Scripture read and opened to our minds, pray, 'Lord, guide our conversations to your glory.' Like dear Laura, who I mentioned earlier, take every opportunity to seek to encourage one another and build one another up in godly ways. Pray for the building up of the people of God for the glory of his name, and, like Laura, earnestly look for personal God-given opportunities to serve him to that end.

Heavenly Father, you have appointed your Son to be the way, the truth and the life, that no one comes to you except through him. Grant us the humility to accept your wisdom, bow the knee to him and live in a way that pleases you. Grant that the power of God may be seen in this place, felt among us and recognised by those among whom we live.

Questions for personal reflection or discussion

1. Have you known men or women like Laura, who could only be described as 'one of God's precious jewels'?

2. 'The Lord God's power is most gloriously seen, not through our ability, skill and confidence, but through our weakness. The kind of weakness that drives us to our knees before God and throws us in total dependence upon his wisdom, enabling and strength . . .' In seeking to honour the Lord, do we know anything of this?

3. In the Corinthian church there were a number of self-confident, self-appointed 'super apostles'. Do we need to guard against such well spoken and very able people who will appear from time to time in our churches? How will we recognise them?

4. 'God's true church is not to be like a cruise liner with a captain, crew and many passengers, but more like a sailing dingy where every person has a part to play.' Are we content to be on a 'cruise to heaven', or before God did we ought to be taking a more active part?

5. 'Like dear Laura, take every opportunity to seek to encourage one another and build one another up in godly ways.' How can we help one another to do this?

The Christian Church in Danger

But when Cephas [Peter] came to Antioch, I opposed him to his face, because he stood condemned. For before certain men came from James, he was eating with the Gentiles; but when they came he drew back and separated himself, fearing the circumcision party. And the rest of the Jews acted hypocritically along with him, so that even Barnabas was led astray by their hypocrisy. But when I saw that their conduct was not in step with the truth of the gospel, I said to Cephas before them all, "If you, though a Jew, live like a Gentile and not like a Jew, how can you force the Gentiles to live like Jews?"

We ourselves are Jews by birth and not Gentile sinners; yet we know that a person is not justified by works of the law but through faith in Jesus Christ, so we also have believed in Christ Jesus, in order to be justified by faith in Christ and not by works of the law, because by works of the law no one will be justified.

Galatians 2 verses 11-16 English Standard Version

Peter and Paul – a small difference with enormous consequences

I would have sooner written a 'soothing little message' but on this occasion we land right in the middle of a robust disagreement!

What was the disagreement all about? After all, Peter and Paul were fellow apostles and they preached the same gospel.

Peter was the first to preach the gospel to the Gentiles. And if you compare what Peter said in Cornelius' house with what Paul preached in Athens, you will find they both called on their hearers to repent – to turn, submit and obey the Lord God and to believe on his Son, the Lord Jesus. And they both declared that God had put his seal on this call and command by raising Jesus from the dead. (Acts 10:34-43 and Acts 17:22-31)

The disagreement was not over the gospel, it was over Peter's actions. Sometimes our actions speak louder than our words, and can even completely undermine our words.

Paul could see that, by what he had done, Peter had undermined the gospel he proclaimed. Peter had at first mixed with and eaten with Gentile believers at Antioch. He had fully accepted them as fellow members of the kingdom of heaven; his believing brothers and sisters in the Lord Jesus – acknowledging that God had done a wonderful work of grace among them, as he had done in Cornelius's house. (Acts 10:44-48)

But, when some Jewish converts, who were steeped their background Jewish teaching that all Gentiles were 'inferior sinners', came down from James in Jerusalem, Peter drew back and would no longer eat with his fellow believers who were Gentiles. It was as if he was suddenly saying, "You non-Jewish people, who are uncircumcised and do not keep the Jewish traditions and ceremonial law, are not 'proper' members of the kingdom of heaven, as we Jews are." Even Barnabas was swept along with this thinking. Paul had to show Peter what he was doing and say, 'You are not being consistent. What you are doing is not right.'

The Revised Standard Version may help us to see this more clearly, 'But when Peter came to Antioch I opposed him to his face, because he stood condemned. For before certain men came from

James, he ate with the Gentiles; but when they came he drew back and separated himself, fearing the circumcision party. And with him the rest of the Jews acted insincerely, so that even Barnabas was carried away by their insincerity. But when I saw that they were not straightforward about the truth of the gospel, I said to Peter before them all, "If you, though a Jew, live like a Gentile and not like a Jew, how can you compel the Gentiles to live like Jews"'.

These Jewish converts who came from Jerusalem, were known as the 'circumcision party' or 'Judaisers'. They taught that to be properly and fully citizens of heaven, Jewish and Gentile believers alike must believe in the Lord Jesus *and* must be circumcised and keep the Jewish traditions, food laws and festivals.

It was as hard for them as it is for us to break free from long-held ways of thinking.

But here was a way of thinking that the apostle Paul had constantly to stand against. For both Jewish people and Gentile people, the essence of being right with God was, and still is, repentance before God and a wholehearted belief in, and life-changing submission to the anointed Son of God, the Messiah, the Lord Jesus, who died in our place; in order that we might be forgiven.

The Pharisees, the Jewish religious leaders, were attempting to win God's favour by their perfect obedience to the law, and had taught the people this same principle; that God's favour is to be won by our merit. The Judaising believers from the circumcision party had imbibed this teaching and 'added' it to belief in the Lord Jesus as Messiah.

The apostle Paul could see that this addition undermined the simple and true gospel of God. The gospel offered something far better. It is a gospel of God's undeserved and unearned grace. A gospel of God's free gift. And it must not be mixed or added to as the Judaisers had done, and as Peter was now doing.

For us, peace with God, forgiveness and a welcome to heaven is not about the merits of our upbringing, our baptism, our decency, or our respectability, or, as the Jewish converts thought, our religious habits, customs and traditions. We can never earn, win or merit forgiveness, peace with God, a place in heaven.

It is not about what we can *do* to win these things. If it was, as Paul writes in this chapter of his letter to the Galatians, Christ would have died to no purpose; died in vain.

It is what the Son of God has *done* for us in laying aside the glory of heaven and becoming a man, showing and teaching us how to live in God's world for God and, supremely, giving his life on the cross in our place, that we – Jew and Gentile alike – might be 'ransomed, healed, restored, forgiven'; made sons and daughters of the Living God.

Peter, by his actions, blurred and compromised this, and so undermined the gospel of God's grace. Paul, clear-thinking as he was, had to confront him and show him what he was doing.

The enormous significance of Paul's bold intervention for ourselves
If the apostle Paul had not publicly confronted Peter, and those who followed his example, what would have been the result?

The Jewish believers from James would have had their way, and if they had persuaded Paul, too, Jewish believers would have kept faith in the Lord Jesus, the Messiah, within the confines of Jewish traditions. The Christian church would never have been born, and faith in Jesus as the Messiah would merely have been a small and despised branch of Judaism.

Peter's action threatened the very existence of what, under the guiding hand of the Lord God, was to become the world-wide Christian church.

The great commission to 'go and make disciples of all nations', recorded on Matthew; or to 'go into all the world and preach the gospel', as Mark records it; or 'that repentance and forgiveness of sins should be preached in his name to all nations' as Luke records Jesus commanding the disciples, would never have been fulfilled.

There would be no non-Jewish church. No world-wide Christian church. No churches, chapels or Christian gatherings in our towns or cities. No local Christian groups. As one believing Christian exclaimed, "It doesn't bear thinking about!"

We have cause to thank God for the insight and holy boldness of the apostle Paul. And this was not just an isolated occasion. Paul constantly suffered at the hands of Jewish people as he faithfully fulfilled the great commission and proclaimed the gospel of God's free grace. He was beaten, imprisoned, stoned and left for dead.

Despite all he suffered, the apostle Paul could write, '. . . the life I now live, I live by faith in the Son of God who loved me and gave himself for me.'

From repentance before God and faith in the Son of God who loved us and gave himself for us, flows peace with God, the hope of everlasting life and the whole of practical godly living.

Heavenly Father, by your Holy Spirit, open our eyes to see the wonder and the simplicity of the gospel of grace. It is not by what we do or have done, but all of your mercy and kindness. It is the free gift of God given to those who truly repent and recognise, believe and submit to the Son of God who loved us and gave himself for us.

Questions for personal reflection or discussion

1. '. . . they were fellow apostles and they preached the same gospel.' Is it sometimes right and necessary for fellow Christians to warn and correct one another?

2. Who was Peter wanting to please as he separated himself from Gentile believers? Can our judgement of what is right before the Lord God sometimes be clouded by wanting to please some other person or group of people? Can you think of particular times or situations when this has happened, or is likely to happen?

3. 'Sometimes our actions speak louder than our words, they can even completely undermine our words.' Can we sometimes be guilty of this?

4. 'It was as hard for them as it is for us to break free from long-held ways of thinking.' Do we sometimes insist that younger Christians conform to our ways. '

5. 'There would be no non-Jewish church. No world-wide Christian church, no churches, chapels or Christian gatherings in our towns or cities. No local Christian groups. As one believing Christian exclaimed, "It doesn't bear thinking about!"' Can you see the enormous significance of the apostle Paul's defence of the 'uncluttered, uncompromised' gospel?

6. Could you say, with the apostle Paul, '. . . the life I now live, I live by faith in the Son of God who loved me and gave himself for me.'?

Righteousness, Peace and Joy

So then each of us will give an account of himself to God. Therefore let us not pass judgement on one another any longer, but rather decide never to put a stumbling block or hindrance in the way of a brother. I know and am persuaded in the Lord Jesus that nothing is unclean in itself, but it is unclean for anyone who thinks it unclean. For if your brother is grieved by what you eat, you are no longer walking in love. By what you eat, do not destroy the one for whom Christ died. So do not let what you regard as good be spoken of as evil. For the kingdom of God is not a matter of eating and drinking but of righteousness and peace and joy in the Holy Spirit. Whoever thus serves Christ is acceptable to God and approved of men. So let us pursue what makes for peace and for mutual upbuilding.

Romans 14:12-19 English Standard Version

For the kingdom of God is not a matter of eating and drinking but of righteousness and peace and joy in the Holy Spirit

First the setting
The apostle Paul was writing to the young and growing Christian church in Rome. He was almost certainly writing from Corinth, where he stayed for about three months during his third missionary journey. Paul wrote to the Roman church to set out clearly the Christian faith, and to guide them in godly living. In this particular

part of his letter, he is urging the Christian believers, despite their differences, to live together with love, mutual care and harmony.

The challenge was not easy, for the believers came from very different backgrounds. They had very different long-held ideas and dearly-loved traditions. They each had 'baggage' they brought to their communal Christian life. Paul mentions some of the very practical difficulties and differences they had to face if they were to live in Christian harmony. He writes about the keeping of special days, the kind of meat, if any, that it was acceptable to eat, and the drinking or abstaining from wine.

The differences were sharp because, for example, Jewish believers were accustomed to drinking wine with their meals and wanted to preserve the memory of Esther at the Feast of Purim, the cleansing of the temple by Judas Maccabaeus at Hanukkah and the escape from Egypt at Passover, and other Jewish festivals and feasts. However, these feasts meant nothing to the formerly pagan Roman believers, whose past life had revolved around their own high days, with feasts of meat offered to idols and all the drunkenness and orgies associated with pagan temple worship. As new believers, some of these Roman Christians were very sensitive about eating meat that had been offered in sacrifice to idols, and knew full well what drunkenness could lead to, and so many of them would not touch either meat or wine.

As God's new people in Christ Jesus, how could people with such different backgrounds possibly manage to live in a God-honouring community? Paul urged the believers in Rome to see that these differences were not central to the faith. On these matters he called them each to make up their own minds before God, and determine not to judge or criticise, or to cause one another to stumble. They were to make every effort to build one another up in godly living. In the apostle Paul's words, 'So let us pursue what makes for peace and for mutual upbuilding.'

In our day, we have what the Roman church did not have. We have the full light of the Old and New Testaments to guide us. And yet, we too may carry 'baggage'. It is not quite as sharp and dramatic as it was among these early believers. Yet some are comfortable with alcoholic drinks and some are not. Some keep church traditions like the season of Lent or eating fish on Fridays and some do not. Some love the old hymns accompanied by an organ, while others cannot tolerate them, preferring modern songs accompanied by a music group. Some freely lift their hands in worship, while others feel very uncomfortable with such outward displays.

Paul wrote to the Christians at Rome about the less important issues, because what really matters is the kingdom of God and its practical expression in and through the Christian community. The kingdom of God is not about keeping our man-made religious rules and traditions, or about our personal scruples, but about 'righteousness, peace and joy in the Holy Spirit'.

Righteousness

The root of the word means 'just' or 'right', and there is an old English spelling of it, 'rightwiseness'; the consistent wisdom to choose that which is just, fair and right. Reflecting how the word is used in Scripture, it is helpful to consider righteousness under three headings, the righteousness of God, our righteousness before him and righteousness of living in the sight of God.

Firstly, the righteousness of God The Lord God is right, just and fair. With confidence, Abraham could plead, 'Shall not the Judge of all the earth do what is right?' The apostle Paul, in 2 Tim 4:8, could write of '. . . the Lord the righteous judge,' and Acts 17:31 records Paul warning the leading men of Athens, 'God . . . has fixed a day on which he will judge the world in righteousness.' This characteristic of righteousness is a reflection of the Lord God's holiness, faithfulness and truthfulness.

Secondly, our righteousness before God By human nature not one of us is counted righteous before him, 'For all have sinned and are falling short of his perfect standard' (Romans 3:23). Or, as the apostle John puts it in 1 John 1:8, 'If we say we have no sin, we deceive ourselves, and the truth is not in us.' However, as the apostle John continues, 'If we confess our sins, he is faithful and just to forgive us our sins and to cleanse us from all unrighteousness.' If we turn and confess our failure to the Lord God, we will find he has made a way by the cross of his Son for us to be forgiven. Despite our failure, in Christ Jesus, we can be 'made' or 'declared' righteous before him.

Finally as believers, the righteousness of godly living This is the challenge of living rightly in the sight of God. If we have been put right with God through true repentance and faith in his Son, we are his new creation, new creatures in Christ Jesus. And we are now called to live lives that reflect being made anew; lives that are pleasing to the Lord God, fulfilling the tasks that he gives us to do in a way that brings honour to him.

For our part, in Ephesians we read, '. . . we are his workmanship, created in Christ Jesus for good works, which God has prepared beforehand, that we should walk in them.' And in Colossians, '. . . walk in a manner worthy of the Lord, fully pleasing to him, bearing fruit in every good work and increasing in knowledge of God.' (Ephesians 2:10 and Colossians 1:10)

We also have the whole of Scripture to show us both good and bad examples, and to teach us by express commandments and by a range of teaching in the Old and New Testaments.

Peace

Peace again has different aspects.

The very nature of the Lord God is peace The writer to the Hebrews concludes with the prayer, 'Now may the God of peace who brought again from the dead our Lord Jesus, the great Shepherd of the sheep, by the blood of the eternal covenant, equip you with everything good that you may do his will, working in you that which is pleasing in his sight, through Jesus Christ, to whom be glory for ever and ever. Amen.' (Hebs13:20-21)

Then our own peace with God Here is a peace that has a sure foundation, and a God-given assurance of its reality. A self-confident feeling of being at peace with God, is not to be trusted if it is merely the fruit of our own feeling or thinking, or if it is founded on what someone else has taught us. Even the 'Church's teaching' is only reliable in so far as it is faithful to Scripture. The only sure foundation is one built on the teaching of the word of God. That means peace with God through our turning away from ungodly ways, and faith in the Son of God. The Lord Jesus plainly stated '. . . I am the way, and the truth, and the life. No one comes to the Father except through me.' (John 14:6) The apostle Peter declared to the religious leaders of his day, who believed that peace with God depended on their own religious obedience, '. . .there is salvation in no one else, for there is no other name under heaven given among men by which we must be saved.' (Acts 4:12) It is through him, the Lord Jesus, that we have both peace with, and access to, God the Father (Romans 5:1-2)

Peace within The third aspect of peace is the peace of God resting on us as we seek to live godly lives in this fallen world. We will all face trials and difficulties, frustrations and delays, sicknesses and sadnesses. As we do so we can trust in the Lord God's care for us and his reassuring hand on our lives. He is in control of all our circumstances. Our Lord promised his disciples his peace despite the tribulations that the world would throw at them, and that he would be with them until the end of the age. (John14:27 and Matthew 28:20)

Jesus also spoke of taking his yoke on us, and as we do so, finding rest, deep peace, as we live in obedience to him. (Matthew 11:28-30)

Peace with one another This is the context in which Paul is writing to the Christians at Rome as he urges them to live at peace despite their differences. Peace with one another flows from peace with God through his Son, an acceptance and wonder at God's love toward us, totally undeserving as we know ourselves to be. From this flows an acceptance and peace within ourselves despite all our failures and wishes to be something other than what we are.

With such inner peace, we can begin to fulfil our God-given calling to be peace-makers. This is peace that reaches out to others in patience, kindness, love, support and forgiveness. Quoting the pagans around him, Tertullian wrote, '"Look," they say, "See how these Christians love one another", for they themselves hate one another.' This is the kind of peace and love Paul was urging the Christians at Rome to discover and put into practice.

Righteousness, peace and joy

The root of the word joy is the same as that of 'rejoice', and Paul defines the joy he is speaking of as *'joy in the Holy Spirit'*. It is not

RIGHTEOUSNESS, PEACE AND JOY

a light and worldly 'happiness' but a God-given, deep well of joy, a constant source of rejoicing springing from knowing that our breath and all our circumstances are safely in the hand of, and under the providential care of, our heavenly Father.

It is the joy of knowing that the Lord God has set his love on us in his Son, the Lord Jesus. Knowing such deep joy, Paul and Silas could sing and pray and rejoice despite being put with their feet in stocks in the dreadful depth of a Philippian prison. (Acts 16:23-25)

And finally it is the joy that comes from being aware of the indwelling Holy Spirit leading and guiding us. Seeing the Lord God's hand on our circumstances, our endeavours and our conversations with other people causes us to be constantly thanking him and rejoicing in him.

The kingdom of God does not have its heart in religious traditions, food, drink or the keeping of special days. These things are secondary. The heart of the matter is righteousness, peace and joy in the Holy Spirit.

Paul wrote to the Christians at Rome to explain these things and to encourage them in godly ways of living.

Heavenly Father, as your Son the Lord Jesus set the hearts of the two disciples walking to Emmaus on fire, burning within them, please thrill us afresh with the wonder of your grace and mercy toward us, and the righteousness, peace and joy in the Holy Spirit that lie at the heart of true faith.

Questions for personal reflection or discussion

1. How many of us would be willing to admit that we bring 'baggage' from our upbringing and customs to the practical outworking of our Christian faith?

2. How easy is it to agree as true Christian believers, and yet have very different understandings on some of the less important issues like our traditions, personal preferences and the way we think things should be done?

3. For ourselves, do we know and rejoice in the things that Paul teaches lie at the heart the kingdom of God.

4. How often are our churches good, even excellent, on the matters that are peripheral, and rather weak concerning the things that lie at the heart of true New Testament Christianity? How can we help one another?

Looking to Jesus

Therefore, seeing we are surrounded by so great a cloud of witnesses, let us also lay aside every weight, and the sin which clings so closely, and let us run with endurance the race that is set before us, looking to Jesus the founder and perfecter of our faith, who for the joy that was set before him endured the cross, despising the shame, and is seated on the right hand of the throne of God.

Hebrews 12:1-2 English Standard Version

Looking to Jesus

'Therefore, seeing we are surrounded by so great a cloud of witnesses . . .' At first glance, we very easily picture thousands of saints and angels looking down from heaven and watching us as we run our earthly race. However, the 'great cloud of witnesses' are not watching us, but bearing witness to the Lord God's faithfulness, grace, upholding power and steadfast love as they faithfully ran their race.

It is easy to overlook the word that connects this chapter with the last. It is there in the original Greek and is translated into English for us as 'therefore'. It means, 'in the light of what has been written, these are the examples to follow'.

It calls us to look at what has been written in Hebrews chapter 11. That chapter is an account of the great heroes of faith who have run the race before us. They are the 'witnesses' or 'martyrs' of the faith – the Greek can mean either. The saints of God described in chapter 11 remained steadfast in their faith, even though some of them 'suffered mocking and flogging, and even chains and imprisonment.'

These verses are laying before us the challenge to be like them, steadfastly living the life of faith, despite the challenges, the sneers and the hurts inflicted on us. It was a challenge to the generation in which the letter was written, and it is a challenge to our generation. Like them we are challenged not to be feeble-minded, faint hearted or tempted to give up. We are to let the example of the heroes of chapter 11 be an encouragement to us and a spur to keep us going, so that we do not let down those who have courageously run the race before us.

How are we to keep going?
'Let us also lay aside every weight, and the sin which clings so closely.' Like a runner in a long distance race we are to put aside or literally 'throw off' everything that would hold us back, hinder us, or weigh us down.

A runner would never dream of competing in an overcoat and heavy boots! And it is for each of us to search and examine ourselves honestly before God and lay aside all those things that would hinder us from wholly following the Lord. For each of us, they will be different.

It is the same with the next challenge, to 'throw off' the sin that so easily entangles. The Greek is literally the 'besetting sin', our personal, secret corruptions and strong inclinations that crop up again and again. Perhaps the constant inclination to escape from a difficult situation by not telling the whole truth. It is good to each ask ourselves, 'What is my besetting sin?' To justify myself, no matter what? To blame other people when things go wrong? To bear grudges? To flare up in anger, or in secret envy or desire? For each of us it will be different and will rear its head again and again. It will entangle us unless we throw it out, or 'throw it off' when our minds first suggest it. I grew up among school friends who were petty thieves, and I joined in. But if you steal, you soon learn to lie, and together they increasingly entangle you. It was not until, on one occasion, the Lord God popped into my head the words 'it is not yours' that I was able to begin to 'throw it off'.

Things that hinder, sins that entangle – throw them off so as to be able to run with endurance the race that is set before us. The Greek for endurance is the word from which we get 'agony'. It implies a struggle which will need both active determination and endurance.

The pattern set by those who have gone before
To our minds, the word 'race' suggests a contest in which we are competing with others. Perhaps a better expression might have been 'to run the course set before us'. For we are not competing with one another in a race, but running the personal course that the Lord God has called us to – with all its individual opportunities and challenges. In that way Luke, in Acts 13:25, records John the Baptist 'finishing his course'. And in his second letter to Timothy, Paul writes of accomplishing or completing his course. (2 Timothy 4:6-8) For each of us our course will be different; different opportunities to bring glory to the Lord God – for some that will be very public – for others quietly and hidden away from the public gaze.

We will have different mountains to climb, rivers to ford and dark valleys to pass through. However each of us is called to run the course God has given us with determined endurance, bearing in mind those godly folk we have known who have faithfully run their course before us, and letting their memory spur us on.

The pattern set by our Lord

The challenge is to run our course, 'looking to Jesus'. The Greek is 'to look away to Jesus' the author and finisher of our faith. To consciously take our eyes off the difficulties, temptations and challenges we face. Overwhelming as they may seem, they are small in comparison with slurs, difficulties and agonies the Lord Jesus suffered on our behalf.

The challenge for us is to keep our eye on him, seeking to please him by running the course and fulfilling the task he has given. Like a runner, keeping an eye on the finishing line, we are to keep an eye on completing the course with joy; aiming to hear our Lord say, 'Well done, good and faithful servant.'

Looking to Jesus the founder, or more helpfully, as older translations have it 'author', of our faith. True faith is a vital new life, the gift of God by his Holy Spirit, secured and made available to us through his Son the Lord Jesus, the author and finisher of our faith. It is the Lord Jesus who laid aside the glory of heaven, humbled himself, became one of us, and throughout his life demonstrated how to walk closely with God our heavenly Father. For our rescue he endured the agony of the cross, and the spite, insults and abuse of the religious leaders, Roman conquerors and ordinary people alike.

He it is whom God raised up and to whom he has given the name above every name. (Philippians 2:9) He is the author and finisher, the perfecter, the one who brings to completion true faith.

Although it is our responsibility 'to run the race', yet at another level the life of a believer from start to finish is all a work of God: Father, Son and Holy Spirit. The apostle Paul wrote, '. . . I am confident of this, that he who began a good work in you will bring it to completion at the day of Jesus Christ.' (Philippians 1:6) And John Newton could sing,

Through many dangers, toils and snares I have already come:
'Tis grace that brought me safe thus far, and grace will lead me home.

'Who for the joy that was set before him endured the cross, despising the shame, and is seated at the right hand of the throne of God'. Here is the final strong encouragement given to us to hold fast and press on. It is the pattern of our Lord himself. The Lord God set before his only Son this course and calling; to rescue and redeem fallen people from every tribe and language and nation and make them sons and daughters of the living God.

The Lord Jesus has redeemed a people for God from every nation. What enabled him to keep going, even through the agony of Gethsemane and Calvary? It was the joy that was set before him on the completion of that great task. In total obedience to his Father, he has completed it and is now risen from the dead and given a name above every name. He is the author and finisher of our faith and is now seated at the right hand of God; and has been given all authority. With his Father he shares the throne of heaven, and governs and reigns over the events of this world.

Here is strong encouragement for those of us still 'running our course'. For the promise is given, that those who remain faithful to the end will 'reign with him', and share with him and with the Father the joy and the glory of heaven.

In conclusion

In these few verses there is great encouragement from the past: the example of the great heroes of faith, 'who through faith held fast.' And great encouragement from the pattern set by our Lord Jesus himself, who for the joy of heaven set before him endured the cross, despising the shame.

The challenge to the Hebrew believers long ago, and to us, is not to fall short, but fervent in spirit and out of gratitude and love, to keep on 'running the race' and serving the Lord. If we hold fast, one day it will be our joy to be with the Lord, the author and finisher of our faith, and among fellow saints in glory.

In the words of the apostle Paul writing to encourage the Corinthian Christians, '. . . be steadfast, unmovable, always abounding in the work of the Lord, knowing that in the Lord your labour is not in vain'. (1 Corinthians 15:58)

Heavenly Father we thank you that you have brought us safely this far. By your grace may we each hold fast to the course that you have set before us, running with patience, courage and determination, and looking to your glorious, anointed Son our Lord Jesus in whose name we ask it.

Questions for personal reflection or discussion

1. Can our Lord's warnings not to make our priority 'the laying up of treasure' (Matthew 6:19-21) or 'the building of bigger barns' (Luke 12:16-21) help us to 'run the race' more freely?

2. Do you have godly close relatives, teachers or friends who have run the race before you?

3. How can the pattern set by our Lord, of being undaunted by the scorn and suffering, inspire you and strengthen your resolve to hold fast?

4. What can true believers look forward to if we do not grow weary or let ourselves be deflected?

5. Can the reminder that we are 'strangers and pilgrims' (Hebrews 11:13) and that '. . . here we have no lasting city' (Hebrews 13:14) help us to 'run the race' with our eyes steadily fixed on being 'with the Lord' in heaven?

The Circumstances of our Lord's Promised Return

Matthew, Mark and Luke all record Jesus' preparation of the disciples for his return. His teaching began with him explaining to the disciples that, despite their awe of the impressive temple that king Herod had built, ". . .there will not be left here one stone upon another that will not be thrown down."

Matthew records that, as Jesus sat on the Mount of Olives, the disciples came to him privately, saying, "Tell us, when these things will be, and what will be the sign of your coming, and of the close of the age?" (Matthew 24:1-3 E.S.V.)

In answer to those questions, Jesus gave a prophetic overview of the near and the distant future – concluding with his own return. From our Lord's description, it becomes clear that his return, the return of the Son of Man, will be in power and great glory, and will be sudden, unexpected, and accompanied by terrifying earthly and cosmic disturbances.

The nearness of the kingdom of God
Our natural modern human assumption is that the kingdom of heaven will be quietly ushered in by universal peace among people. But that is not what our Lord said.

He said, 'There will be signs in the sun, the moon, and the stars, and on the earth distress among nations confused by the roaring of the sea and the waves. People will faint from fear and foreboding of what is coming upon the world, for the powers of the heavens will be shaken. Then they will see the Son of Man coming in a cloud with power and great glory. Now when these things begin to take place, straighten up and raise your heads, because your redemption is drawing near.' (Luke 21:25-28) The 'Son of Man' is the title Jesus often used of himself.

The Lord Jesus warned that the coming of the Son of Man will be associated with all the distress and confusion foretold by God's prophets, Isaiah, Joel, Amos and Zephaniah, concerning the 'Day of the Lord.' Isaiah spoke of the sun, the moon and the stars; the whole created order being in great confusion and commotion. As Jesus warned, men and women will be filled with overwhelming apprehension; fainting for fear of the future.

Illustrated by Jesus' parable of the appearance of the leaves on the fig tree, and other trees, the disciples were solemnly called to take careful note of the signs of human history, and so be prepared for what he warned would be the terrifyingly violent and fearful end of this present evil age.

". . . when you see these things taking place, you know that the kingdom of God is near . . . Heaven and earth will pass away, but my words will not pass away." (Luke 21:29-33)

The earth-shaking days of which Jesus spoke are clearly not local events, but the final days of the world as we know it. These awesome and awful world-wide happenings are the 'birth pains' that will herald the approach of the beginning of the Messiah's glorious reign.

The timing of our Lord's return
It is clear from the New Testament that the early church lived in eager expectation that Jesus' promised return would take place

within their own lifetime. Two thousand years later we are still called to heed our Lord's words, and to be constantly on our watch and prepared.

In every generation there have been good folk who, touched by war, epidemic, fire or flood, conclude and proclaim that 'this is the end.' But, again, the Lord did warn, "And when you hear of wars and tumults, do not be terrified, for these things must first take place, but the end will not be at once." (Luke 21:9) Rather, our Lord warned us to take careful note of the coming together of many world-wide and world-convulsing events and disasters that together present an overwhelming threat to humanity's very existence.

Disciples are nowhere encouraged to work out a timetable for the return of the Son of Man. Kenneth Bailey notes that, 'Some believers in every century have held the firm conviction that they were living in the last days . . . Christians in every age are encouraged to live expectantly and at the same time never to presume to read the mind of the Father as regards the timing of the end of all things.'

What is the relevance of this to us?
These great upheavals are signs to summon humanity to turn to the Lord God and to honour both him and his anointed Son. The great question is, 'Will we acknowledge our failure to honour and obey the God in whose hand is our very existence? Or will we continue to ignore and treat our Maker with contempt until the very last day?' On 'that day', every eye will see God's anointed Son, the Son of Man who lived on earth in great humility as one despised and rejected, return in great glory and majesty as Lord and Judge of every one of us.

Those who have ignored and failed to honour him will face his just judgement. To them his appearance must inevitably bring great terror. But to those who have humbled themselves before him and received him, and who obey him, and continue to serve him as his faithful servants as they wait and watch for his return, the return of the Son of Man will bring awe and wonder, and great joy.

The ongoing call to be ready
As the trees bursting into leaf are a clear sign that summer is near, so disciples then, and now, are called to watch the signs, and to be ready for times of great testing, and ready for the return of the Son of Man.

Matthew also records, in chapter 24 verses 6-14, our Lord's warning that as his return approaches, there will be famines, earthquakes, international wars, and a general hatred and persecution of Jewish people, and of Gentile, Bible-believing Christian people. All these things will be taking place in such an increasingly Godless, and spiritually-freezing atmosphere, that the love of many both for the Lord and for one another will grow cold.

The big question to ask is, 'Could we be living at the beginning of days like these?'

The unbelieving world will always regard Jesus' warnings as 'fairy tales', but despite clever weaving of words or sneers, it is clear that Christian believers are called to hold fast to our Lord's words, for only then shall we be prepared.

'Be on guard so that your hearts are not weighed down with dissipation and drunkenness and the worries of this life, and that day does not catch you unexpectedly, like a trap. For it will come upon all who live on the face of the whole earth. Be alert at all times, praying that you may have strength to escape all these things that will take place, and to stand before the Son of Man.' (Luke 21:34-36)

These words summon us to walk closely with the Lord, and not to let the all-consuming cares, concerns and pleasures of this world make us like drunken people; dull-headed and sleepy. They call us to beware of all that would quench a close spiritual walk with the Lord God and his Son the Lord Jesus. We are to keep close to him so that we may each be found faithful and obedient, watching and ready, rather than overtaken and trapped. Our consistent, ultimate aim and joy should be to 'stand before the Son of Man', and hear words from our Lord such as these: "Well done good and faithful servant . . . enter into the joy of your Lord".

On the wall of the church where I served as Rector, there is a wall tablet or monument with a text from Luke chapter 12, verse 40, 'Be ye also ready; for at such a time as ye think not, the Son of Man cometh.' The Lord warned that he will return at an hour we do not expect. But will we be ready? Will I be ready? Will you be ready? Will we be prepared?

Heavenly Father, give us ears to hear and minds and hearts to heed these most serious words of your Son.

We pray for Jewish people, both scattered throughout the nations and gathered in their homeland, to whom these words were first addressed.

We pray, too, for the people of the Gentile nations, including our own, the vast majority of whom are completely unaware of the seriousness of warnings such as these.

Father, it is not your will that any should perish but that all should come to repentance. We plead with you that in your mercy you would send a world-wide spiritual revival. Cause us to turn, repent, believe, take heed, watch, pray and be faithfully about your business – and so be found ready for the return of your glorious and anointed Son.

Questions for personal reflection or discussion

1. 'Our natural modern human assumption is that the kingdom of heaven will be quietly ushered in by universal peace among people. But that is not what our Lord said.' Do you think that we modern Christians are all but asleep and in danger thinking this way?

2. 'From our Lord's description, it becomes clear that his return . . . will be in power and great glory, and will be sudden, unexpected and accompanied by terrifying earthly and cosmic disturbances. If our Lord's words concerning his return are so serious, why do we so rarely speak of them, or hear sermons and talks warning us, and helping us to be prepared for our Lord's return?

3. 'It is clear that the New Testament that the early church lived in eager expectation that Jesus' promised return would take place within their own lifetime. Two thousand years later we are still called to heed our Lord's words, and to be constantly on our watch and prepared.' Are we? Should we be? How can we be?

4. 'The unbelieving world will always regard Jesus' warnings as 'fairy tales', but despite clever weaving of words or sneers, it is clear that Christian believers are called to hold fast to our Lord's words, for only then shall we be prepared.' Without being anxious or fretting, how can we be quietly and steadily prepared?

5. The Lord warned that he will return at an hour we do not expect. But will we be ready? Will I be ready? Will you be ready? Will we be prepared?

About the Cover Image, the Author and related Publications

The Book Cover
The cover image is from an overland expedition to the Middle East and Jerusalem undertaken by a group of students in 1964. It is of one of us on a shepherd's donkey lent for a few moments by a passing group of shepherds as they brought their very large flock of sheep to safety for the night.

The Author
Born in Great Malvern, Worcestershire, England, John Belham has a scientific background, but for most of his life has had the privilege of serving with some very wonderful people, first in suburban ministry, then as Rector of a group of country parishes, and more recently assisting with city ministry. Married with four grown-up children, he delights in the Lord God – his word, his people and his creation.

His spiritual journey
A Praying Teacher, a Crystal Diode and Winter Wheat
A twelve year old lad, headphones on, oblivious to the world, sprawled out at the top of the stairs, right in the way – fiddling with a very simple radio receiver; a crystal set. Will it work? Only if he can get the little wire to touch on the crystal at such a point that it makes a one way electrical gateway; a diode. He tried this way and

that, between times adjusting the tuning condenser to search for the different radio stations. Nothing. Then, suddenly, he hit the spot. The little wire, known as the cat's whisker, was now making contact with a 'sweet spot' and the whole device sprang to life.

A live broadcast filled my headphones and ears. Was it music? Was it the news, the weather or a discussion? No, it was none of these. It was a preacher preaching!

Was it the preaching or the fact that the little, home-built radio set worked? I don't know. But I listened right to the end and, when it finished, determined that I wanted to hear more. The preacher's talks were being relayed by telephone line to a local church, and I asked my Dad to take me to hear him. No razzmatazz, no great build up, nothing visual, just a song and a talk. But through it the Lord God spoke as clearly as any voice, 'John, it is you I want.' I nudged my Dad but he was quite unmoved and, in talking with the minister of the church we attended as a family, he was assured, 'Don't worry, of course he'll soon get over it.' I would have done, but for Miss Gibbs, a teacher at school who taught both English and what was known in those far off days as 'Scripture'. With hindsight, that lady plainly not only taught her youngsters but coveted them for the Lord and prayed for them. It was Miss Gibbs who recognised that the Lord God had begun a work in my life and patiently encouraged me to begin to read the Bible.

The little seed of faith began to grow, springing up like wheat sown in the mild autumn weather. However, as a family, we moved away very soon after that and the next ten years proved to be a very severe spiritual winter, with little or no Christian fellowship or encouragement. Spiritual life withered away, like the wheat in winter; yellowed and to all appearances dead and finished. Until, that is, a spiritual springtime in my twenties saw faith rekindled and the winter-sown wheat vigorously sprouting.

It was the second, tiny 'chance happening' under the hand of God. David, a friend in the local actors' club, offered me a lift.

He was going to a church in 'West Ken', which I took to be a few miles down the road in Kent. It wasn't, it was in Kensington – yet here was the vital Christianity I hadn't encountered since a young schoolboy.

After a while, I was even willing to heed a long-known, nagging suspicion that the Lord God would have me 'turn my collar round' – to become a Christian minister. It culminated in a prayer that you won't find in any prayer book, 'O.K. Lord, you win.' My employer's reaction astonished me, 'But of course,' as did my landlady's, 'Yes, it is about time you stopped messing about.'

I have had the privilege of marrying, bringing up a family and working for many years among some wonderful people in both city and rural ministry. Day by day I remain thrilled and amazed by the gracious dealing, mercy and love of the Lord God, and just so grateful for his kindness, mercy and patience with such a difficult and wayward son. Yet an adopted son I find myself to be, and one rescued and redeemed by the precious cross of his Son. In the apostle Paul's words, I gladly confess, 'I live by faith in the Son of God who loved me and gave himself for me.' 'Of course, he'll soon get over it.' But, by the grace of the Lord God, I haven't yet, and that was said over sixty years ago!

As you can see, it is the story of God's gracious dealing with a rebellious and unwilling child and could well be summed up as it began – 'saved by a cat's whisker'.

Exploring and Applying the Lord's Prayer
A Prayer to Change the World

'In the setting of great thankfulness to my heavenly Father, the phrases of the Lord's Prayer became such a precious spur to worship and guide and compass for life; that I had to scribble a little book on it to share its jewels with others.'

Given understanding and a willingness to take it to heart, the Lord's Prayer will not only teach us to pray, it will revolutionise the way we think and the way we live. It is so much more than a gentle murmur. It is a prayer to change the world – beginning with those who pray it.

This is a book highlighting the practical out-working of this greatest of prayers. Chapter by chapter you are invited to explore and apply each phrase, as if you were exploring the rooms of a great mansion. There are questions for personal reflection or discussion.

It is as if you are personally invited to spend time as an honoured guest in a great house. You have complete freedom to enjoy the magnificence of the splendid rooms, but also have freedom to visit the more practical rooms – the kitchens, store rooms, even the bathrooms and security rooms. You are free to meet with members of the household, to admire the furnishings, to pause at the windows and enjoy both the lovely gardens and the fine sweeping views across the estate.

Such, and infinitely greater, is the wonderful invitation given to every disciple within the lines of the Lord's Prayer. Rather than a prayer to be repeated, it is more like a magnificent house to explore.

'Packed with a very great deal of Christian devotion and Biblical teaching . . . with a pastoral touch throughout.'

    Richard Bewes, a former Rector of All Souls Church, Langham Place, London

ISBN 978-0-9537489-4-5

For further details and to hear the accompanying podcasts visit https://www.lords-prayer.co.uk or search online 'Exploring and applying the Lord's Prayer'.

Exploring and Applying the Parables of Jesus found in the Gospel of Luke

For those with ears to hear, the parables of Jesus speak as sharply and relevantly today as they did 2000 years ago. If you are willing to be stirred and challenged – as the first hearers were – read on. The author invites you to an exploration of each parable in its setting, followed by questions for personal reflection or group discussion.

The book is not intended to be a specialist or academic text but has been written for a wider readership of Christian people. It is currently associated with a website, *exploring and applying the parables*, where podcasts of a number of the parables are offered.

ISBN 978-0-9537489-2-1

'This is a book to read if you want to gain a deeper understanding of the parables taught by Jesus.'

Dr. John Clements, Pastor of the Old Meeting House Congregational Church and author of *Strangers and Pilgrims on the Earth*.

Exploring and Applying the Parables

The Parables of Jesus found only in the Gospels of Matthew and Mark

This book continues the series begun in *Exploring and Applying the Parables of Jesus found in the Gospel of Luke*. The aim is to explore each parable in its original setting and then apply its teaching to our current situation in the world today. Like the earlier volume, the book is not intended to be an academic text, but a book for group or personal consideration. Each parable is followed by questions for personal reflection or group discussion.

ISBN 978-0-9537489-5-2

www.ingramcontent.com/pod-product-compliance
Lightning Source LLC
Chambersburg PA
CBHW072042290426
44110CB00014B/1556